Luke Nicoli, co-writer on this book with Kevin Phillips, is a freelance football journalist, having been Features Editor at *Shoot* magazine between 1998 and 2000. He started his career at Collings Sport, where he covered football for *Shoot, Match* and *90 Minutes,* and motor racing for the *Daily Telegraph.* He joined *Match* magazine in 1994 as News Editor, before moving to *Shoot* four years later. Luke also reports for the *Sunday Mirror* and appears regularly on ITV2 and cable channel Nickelodeon. He has known Kevin since his schooldays in Stevenage, where they played football together.

STRIKINGLY DIFFERENT
KEVIN PHILLIPS
with LUKE NICOLI

CollinsWillow

An Imprint of HarperCollins*Publishers*

Dedicated to the memory of my father, Ray.
My guiding light, without whom
there would be no story to tell.

First published in hardback 1999
by CollinsWillow
an imprint of HarperCollins*Publishers*
London

First published in paperback 2000

New and revised edition

© Kevin Phillips 2000

1 3 5 7 9 8 6 4 2

A CIP catalogue record for this book is
available from the British Library

ISBN 0 00 218962 3

Printed and bound in Great Britain by Clays Ltd, St Ives plc

The HarperCollins website address is:
www.fireandwater.com

Photographic acknowledgments
Action Images: 6b, 14tr; **Allsport:** 5t, 5b, 7t, 7b, 8, 12tl, 12tr, 12b,
13b, 14b, 15t; **Bonneys:** 11b, 15b, 16; **Empics:** 4t, 4b, 6t, 9, 10t, 11t.
All other photographs courtesy of Kevin Phillips.

Contents

ACKNOWLEDGMENTS

I would like to thank Luke for all his efforts in helping put this book together in such a short space of time. Thanks also go out to Phil Smith and the staff at First Artists, Peter Reid and all the Sunderland playing staff, Glenn Roeder for giving me my chance at Watford, Ian Allinson for doing the same at Baldock and, of course, all my family and friends. But I'd like to save the last word for my wife, Julie: thank you for all your support and love these past couple of years.

Kevin Phillips

I'd like to thank my fiancee Tanya for her understanding during the writing of this book, my parents for all their support and encouragement, Angelo and the staff at the Poseidon Hotel in Kos, Ed and Ann at Watford FC, the staff at SHOOT magazine, Tim Collings, Chris Hunt, Andy Winter, Nikki Clarkson, Julie for the Red Bull and sandwiches, Tom Whiting at publishers Collins Willow, and, of course, Kevin for his time, co-operation and honesty – here's to further success in the Premiership, you deserve it.

Luke Nicoli

CHAPTER ONE

Saints, Sunblest and Success

Professional football is a cut-throat business at the best of times. But when you've scored goals all your life and are then converted to a defender overnight, your chances of making the grade are limited even further.

That's the situation I found myself in as a YTS trainee at Southampton. Having scored goals throughout my junior career, it was Saints scout Bob Higgins who took me to The Dell after seeing my goalscoring ability one day when I was turning out for North Herts Schools. He saw something he liked. A little spark, a good turn of pace and an eye for goal. And I was on my way to fulfilling my lifetime's ambition... professional footballer and goalscoring legend at that!

But life's never that simple. After two years attending Southampton's School of Excellence at their local centre in Harlow and having skippered the side to the Gothia

Cup in Sweden which, incidentally, we won twice, it was make or break time. Boss Chris Nicholl was obviously impressed with what he saw in this slight teenager and it was enough to earn me a two-year YTS contract. I remember the date clearly, 1 July 1988. Yet another step towards that golden dream but, as it turned out to be, a million miles away.

The season was two months old but this keen 16-year-old had already hit a brick wall. Saints coach Dave Merrington was not over-impressed, especially with my appearance. 'Kevin,' I clearly recall him saying. 'At this level, I don't think you're cut out to be a striker. You've got the talent, you just haven't got the build for it.' Those words were hard to take, especially as I still had a long way to go before I reached my full growing potential. But I was half expecting it. I hadn't broken into the team and just as I was about to turn away from Dave and skulk back to training, he gave me a lifeline. 'But,' he added, 'you're good coming onto the play instead of having your back to the game, so what about a run out at right-back?'

Right-back? That's where the crap kid who can't play the game usually ends up, isn't it? Well, it was when I was at school, but you've got to remember that this kid was desperate to make it. Who knows, I might have a blinder. This could still be my route into the big time. Then again, it could leave me on the path to oblivion.

The early signs were good, much better than I had anticipated. I took the job on and ended up playing the remainder of the season in the number two shirt. Not only that, weight-training saw my 5ft 4in frame growing

8

with every day! And the vibes were good. I started the second, crucial year of my YTS still at right-back and all thoughts of becoming the Saints' new Alan Shearer had gone right out of my head. I might have cleaned his boots but I was a defender now.

Things were going so well, in fact, that I'd even broken into the reserve side. A run out at Ipswich's Portman Road was followed by a couple of games at The Dell. 'This is it,' I thought. 'I've made it.' Well, when you're playing with established first-teamers at 17, you've got to be confident. But, as I was later to find out both on and off the pitch, life has a habit of slapping you in the face when you're least expecting it.

Although life as a YTS footballer lasts for two years, it's the month of February in the second season that is critical. That's the date of destiny for all trainees and an occasion I'll never forget.

I can remember it so vividly. All of us hopefuls were summoned to the away dressing room at The Dell, and when your name is called, you meet your date with destiny or, in our case, a long walk to the boss's room to see Mr Nicholl.

As I made that journey, I passed a couple of lads in tears. Two years of hard graft had gone down the pan for them. But I promised myself to remain calm. If I'd earned myself a professional contract, all well and good. If I hadn't, then there was no point getting worked up. I couldn't change the gaffer's mind for him.

But that's not to say I wasn't nervous. I was shaking, trembling, in fact. Let's not forget I was still a boy. When I see 16-year-old apprentices today, they all appear so confident, so wise. But ten or so years ago, I was just a baby. I was a boy hoping to enter a man's world.

The moment of truth had arrived. I opened the door and entered the gaffer's office for the first time. It looked massive, and I appeared so small in comparison. But before I'd made myself comfortable, the killer blow was struck.

'I won't beat around the bush, Kevin. We've decided to release you,' said Nicholl.

'I think you still need a couple more years' experience before you can enter the professional game. You need to build yourself up more. Get stronger. But, I have to be fair and say that you came very close. If I didn't have Jason Dodd and Jeff Kenna ahead of you, we'd have offered you a year's contract. Sorry, son.'

Of course I stood there dazed, absolutely gutted. But almost immediately, I was filled with determination. One man's opinion wasn't going to stop me fulfilling my dream.

'I'm going to prove you wrong. I'm going to make it somewhere,' was my response.

'I hope you do son, I hope you do,' he said as I turned towards the door.

I doubt he thought he'd hear of me again. He'd probably heard the same line one hundred times over.

All I wanted to do now was get packed and get the hell out of town. Well, what was the point, I wasn't wanted. But I stayed for another six weeks and completed my preliminary coaching badge as well as picking up my final wage packet of £136, which at the time seemed far more important.

Then it was back home to the arms of Mum and Dad in my home town of Stevenage. Of course I was devastated but this newly-found determination was a feeling which I'd never really experienced before. All I ever wanted to do was become a professional footballer. But finding a club which wanted me was another matter entirely.

With the help of my landlord in Southampton, Mike Barnard, letters were sent out to all the clubs in the south of England, informing them that this skilful, quick, strong, intelligent full-back had, er, just been released from Southampton. Surely someone would take me after a CV like that. Barnet? Southend maybe?

I did, in fact, receive two replies – from Charlton and Peterborough – but both had taken their full quota of players for the year. I was the forgotten man of football and I hadn't even made it yet. The dream was dying, professional football was on the backburner for now.

And as an 18-year-old, I needed cash. My mates had already been picking up what seemed like hefty pay packets for two years and I was the skinflint. I wanted decent clothes, I wanted a night on the town but I had to pay for it, and I had my Mum Sue to thank for putting me on the right track.

At the time she was a supervisor in the offices of the local Sunblest bread factory and with a twist of an arm, I was on the payroll in no time at all, as a part-time warehouse boy. One moment, I'm rubbing shoulders with legends like Mark Wright and Peter Shilton, the next I'm loading crusty loaves onto the back of a lorry. Oh, what glamour!

'Just think of the cash,' I kept saying to myself and I wasn't to be disappointed. One month and what seemed like 1000 hours later I picked up £700 for my troubles. And not only that, it was cash in hand. I could hardly contain myself and when I got home I remember just throwing the whole lot up in the air in my living room as if I'd just won the lottery. At last I was sorting myself out. Now all I needed was my football back.

In a strange sort of way, Sunblest too helped me back on my footballing path to glory and it was good old Mum who came to my rescue again.

Someone she knew at the factory was a friend of the former Arsenal and Luton striker Ian Allinson, who was now manager of Beazer Homes League side Baldock Town. Another twist of an arm and I'm travelling the short journey up the A1 for a trial.

Ian had, of course, heard of me from my junior days where I scored goals for my club side Fairlands FC. What he didn't know was that Kevin Phillips was now a wannabe defender.

I did enough to impress until I was struck with a case of deja-vu. For the first couple of months I was struggling to get in the team. I was finding it difficult to make the jump into men's non-league football, where anything goes, including your legs if your opponent can stretch far enough!

This right-back venture wasn't happening either. And it took a twist of fate for me, and my boss, to see the light. It was the moment that kick-started my career – a match against Burnham FC.

Ian was struggling to field a side and I was asked

whether I'd like to play up front for the game. I took little persuading and 90 minutes later I was a two-goal hero and went on to notch another 16 times that season. I felt back where I belonged. Of course I wasn't a right-back and this was proof in itself.

I was at last enjoying my football again, while off the field I had moved on, too – into the glamour business of delivering radiator boilers and copper tubes around the Home Counties. Not that I was complaining. I was picking up £200 a week at Baldock as well as earning a wage. Things couldn't be better and now I was the envy of my mates.

As every footballer will tell you, when you're feeling confident, anything's possible. I was now a crowd favourite among our 200 die-hard fans and went on to score 35 goals in my second season. The name Phillips was back and scouts from Millwall, Luton and Barnet were soon on my case. Barnet boss Ray Clemence did in fact give me a trial but opted to play me right-midfield. A big mistake on his part but he must have had some fun watching a headless chicken running around the pitch at Underhill!

The taste for the professional game had returned. I felt on top of the world, having the top boys watching. 'Just why didn't they give me a go when I left Southampton?' was all I could think. Anyway, that was in the past. I had to play for today and 22 goals in the first three months of my third season was fairytale stuff. Surely I deserved another chance now.

Watford boss Glenn Roeder certainly thought so and having watched me play one cold Tuesday night against

Fisher Athletic, I was invited for a trial. I must admit that I didn't perform on the night, but managed to score. Glenn had seen enough. I was phoned by new Baldock boss Bob Eagles on the Friday – Ian had been sacked for a slump in results the previous season – and went for a week's trial the following Monday.

At this point, my pay packet was in the hands of Dixons, whom I was working for to earn some cash for Christmas. They didn't need much persuading to give me the time off.

This was my big chance. It was now December 1994, four years since I was shown the door at The Dell. But those same nerves were there when I turned up for training at Watford's Stanmore training ground. I took to the pitch at 10.30 am and was back inside by 12 noon.

'Is that it?' I said to Glenn. 'What time are we back in this afternoon?'

He just laughed and sent me home. I was living the Life of Reilly and wanted more of it. I was home by 1 pm, and could even have put in a couple of hours at Dixons if I'd wanted to!

That first day was just a breaking-in period. The big test came on Tuesday with a reserve game against Chelsea at Vicarage Road. I was back amongst it, and in a big way. I was starting the game and coming head-to-head with the likes of David Rocastle, Kevin Hitchcock, Paul Furlong, David Lee and Eddie Newton. These were players that I'd grown up watching on television. 'Rocky' was a big favourite of mine as a kid when I used to watch him from the terraces at Arsenal. I couldn't believe I was up against *him*, an England international.

Baldock seemed a million miles away but this was where I wanted to be, so I had to make the most of it.

The final whistle was greeted with relief. I hadn't scored but felt I made a few good runs and showed nice touches. In truth, I found the pace quick and I got caught with the ball a couple of times. I didn't have a shot at goal – and would that prove vital?

I was given Wednesday off but the day was spent going over the game in my mind. 'Had I done enough?' 'Should I have scored?' – just two questions I kept asking myself over and over again.

Thursday was spent training and I knew that Friday would be decision day – a day that could ultimately shape the rest of my life.

Believe it or not, we played rugby that day! Our training ground was waterlogged so we went to Cassiobury Park in Watford and the lads ended up going hammer and tongs at each other with the ball in their hands. They all seemed to be enjoying it but not me. This was my last chance to shine. How the hell could I? Obviously the manager had already made his mind up. Back to Baldock and back to bloody Dixons for me.

As I got changed, Glenn brought me to one side for the gut-wrenching news, or so I thought. 'I still haven't made my mind up,' was his assessment. 'We've got Millwall on Monday at the New Den. Will Dixons give you another day off?'

Did I really need to answer that? I was in the last-chance saloon. It was all or nothing.

We lost the game 2–0 and heads were down, including mine. I thought I had played better than the Chelsea game, but had the result overshadowed Glenn's opinion of me?

The feelings this time were every bit as nerve-jangling as that fateful day in Chris Nicholl's office. I was pulled out of the dressing room and into Millwall's away dugout for the verdict. Fingers were crossed as Glenn said the words 'Two year contract'. I couldn't believe it. I was in ecstasy. I didn't know whether to laugh or cry. But after nine years of trying, I had achieved my lifetime's ambition. I had become a professional footballer. I had made it, second time around.

The first phonecall I made was to Mum and Dad, who were absolutely delighted. Then it was a meeting with Glenn two days later to discuss my first professional contract. Obviously I had no agent at this point, so my Baldock boss Bob acted as my advisor. We all met at the Swallow Hotel in Waltham Abbey on 12 December, but the meeting was irrelevant. I would have signed for anything, that's what becoming a pro meant to me.

My first contract turned out to be £300 a week with a £7,500 signing on fee. Small money indeed, in today's world of millionaire footballers, and I even had to take a pay cut from what I was earning at Dixons. I was signed for £10,000, rising to £35,000 after appearances. I was in dreamland.

Once I'd returned to planet earth my first aim was to get myself in shape and then aim to play out the remainder of the season in the reserves. But could I make the step up? Was I capable of mixing with the elite at Vicarage Road? The early signs were not good.

My goalscoring return was a paltry one goal in six

games and the local press were soon on my case. 'IS HE A WASTE OF MONEY?' I remember them saying. That hurt, but as a professional footballer I had to get used to the press and fast.

It wasn't just the journalists who were on my case. I could sense that a few of the Watford players were uncertain of my ability. Let's not forget that I'd made a major leap. After all, I hadn't even come from the Vauxhall Conference – but two notches below that.

I was feeling down, no two ways about it, but Watford's two wily old pros – Nigel Gibbs and Gary Porter – were soon lifting my spirits with words of comfort and encouragement. They told me to keep my head up because they'd seen enough in me to suggest that I could become a regular first-teamer. I believed that too because if I didn't, I might as well have packed up on the spot.

But before I even had a chance to put a run together in the reserves, my whole world was turned upside down in an instant. It was a cold wet Tuesday night in February 1995, Sunderland ironically were the visitors and Kevin Phillips had been selected to make his first-team debut.

Shock was the first emotion I felt. My record was not the best, but I was set to make my debut as a professional footballer. I had found out that I was playing the night before the game, which gave me time to prepare. My entire family came down for the game and I was in a dreamworld. I don't think I slept a wink the night beforehand, just going through the game before it had even taken place. I just kept saying to myself over and over again to keep things simple and everything else would fall into place. But talk is cheap, I had to go out there and do it.

As kick-off came, it was me going into the first-team changing room, ready to play. I'd seen it time and time again at Southampton, but this time it was the Watford trainees who were looking on in the tunnel, waiting to watch the game on the sidelines.

I was nervous, no question about it, but I just got quietly changed, and focused on the game in hand. As the referee's buzzer went, it was time to go. My date with destiny had arrived. As soon as I had crossed over that white line, I was a Watford player and had a full appearance to my name. That made me so proud. I had made it. Everything felt perfect.

Although this was the most important moment of my life, it was also the greatest feeling of my life. In fact, the only thing that spoilt it was the horrendous Vicarage Road pitch, but getting my boots muddy was a small price to pay. Unfortunately, we came up against a very hard working side in Sunderland and went on to lose to a Craig Russell goal, but I felt I did myself justice. I managed to play out my dream in everything but result and goalscoring winner in the final minute! I kept it simple, didn't try to do anything too flash and I had a couple of good efforts at goal. The crowd could also see that I was a busy, lively striker and they got behind me from the very start. I couldn't have really asked for more and I felt I did well. And Glenn Roeder was obviously impressed.

I remained in the side for the final 15 games of the season and scored nine goals. Of course the highlight was scoring my first, an effort I drilled in against Swindon, but things were also happening to me off the pitch. People were coming up to me at the ground and asking for autographs. Others were approaching me out in Watford. This was my first taste of stardom and I liked it. I even had a chat with Elton John, Mr Watford. In my eyes he is a legendary figure in pop music and I was nervous when I met him. But to him, I was just as important. I was a Watford striker, one of the players whom he enjoyed watching and that made me feel good.

Kevin Phillips had arrived and if there were doubts in my team-mates' minds, I had their full respect by the time the season came to a close. I had paid back my transfer fee and was rewarded with an improved, longer contract. There was no turning back. Or was there?

It's an old cliché, but as I've said, football is full of ups and downs and it has a habit of kicking you in the stomach when you least expect it. And just as I'd begun to make a name for myself, my world fell apart.

I lost my Dad Ray that summer after he suffered a heart attack. I was shattered, absolutely devastated, like any son would be. I find it difficult to explain just what my father meant to me.

But for him, I wouldn't be in the position I am in today. He was the one who encouraged me all the way. He was the one who, even in my Baldock days, stopped me going clubbing on a Friday night with my mates, just so that I would be in tip-top condition for the game the next day. I only did it all for Dad and when I lost him, I wanted to pack it all in. I wanted to quit playing football.

It even got to the point where I phoned Glenn Roeder

to tell him that I didn't want to play anymore. Of course I was in shock, but this was what I felt. Glenn, however, was a massive help. He told me that time is a great healer and that life goes on. 'Do it for your Dad' was what he said. And as the days and weeks passed, that was the right thing to do. Determination is the theme which runs through this book and now I had another reason to go all the way to the top. I wanted Dad to be proud of me and I wanted to succeed for him.

When I look at my career, my one great regret is that my Dad has missed so much – playing for Sunderland, scoring so many goals and, ultimately, playing for England. But I know that he is looking down on me with a smile and still guiding me and it is wonderful to know that he saw me make my debut that night against Sunderland. I know it was the proudest moment of his life and I'm just so pleased that I managed to put such a big smile on his face.

I did return for pre-season and soon got into the process of negotiating my new, improved contract. Of course Dad wasn't around for guidance now but Bob – who is an accountant by trade – came with me to thrash out a deal with Roeder. With the goals I'd scored the previous season, I thought I was worth at least £1,000 a week, but the answer I got was a straight 'piss off!' from the boss. It caused a bit of friction between us for a while, but when I reflected on the situation and realised that I was just a baby in professional footballing terms, I knew I was being stupid. I backed down and everyone was happy.

Now it was on with the business of football. Having

finished seventh in my first season, we were aiming for the play-offs that season and a possible crack at the big time. Again, I was scoring regularly and was, amazingly, joined in attack by at least five partners throughout the season: Peter Beadle, Kerry Dixon, Mickey Quinn, Paul Wilkinson and young Gifton Noel-Williams.

Not that I was complaining. There are three experienced old heads in that list, from whom I learnt a great deal. 'Wilko', in particular, was a big help to me. He was big and strong and I thrived on his flick-ons. Having a big man as partner seemed to bring the best out of me, which I was also to discover when I moved to the north east.

But although I was scoring goals quite freely, the team was struggling quite badly. To this day, I have never been able to put my finger on the reason, because we had more or less the same squad as the previous season. Things came to a head just after Christmas when we were hammered 4–0 at Crystal Palace. I was injured and didn't play that day and the next morning I received a call at home from the gaffer informing me that he'd been sacked. It was another huge blow I had to recover from for Glenn was the man who gave me my big chance. I will always be grateful to him. I learnt such a lot from him too during his time at Watford and now he was gone. I was left alone again but we still keep in contact, even to this day and, thankfully, Glenn soon returned to football, first with Glenn Hoddle's England set-up and more recently on the coaching staff at West Ham.

There was plenty of speculation as to who would replace Glenn. We'd heard rumours that former Watford boss Graham Taylor was the strong favourite, having recently been sacked by Wolves, and those rumours turned to concrete fact within a few days.

Now this was all new to me. A new manager. He hadn't brought me into the game from non-league. So what if he didn't fancy me? What if he thought I wasn't up to the task? I had to start all over again, but when I spoke to my team-mates I soon realised that they were having exactly the same thoughts, and that put me at ease.

But I still had to show the new man what I could do. Thankfully, he stuck with me and my first appearance under his wing came in a league game against Ipswich. I played well and afterwards he dragged me to one side and said: 'You're a good player and if you do what I say, you can go to the very top'. That was what I wanted to hear from a man of his stature and credentials. I felt great. I felt wanted again. But just like before, yet another obstacle was thrown in my face.

I'd scored 12 goals up until that March and was the club's leading goalscorer, but on the fourth day of that month, I was to suffer the first of two very long and very worrying injuries that put more than one question mark over my career.

I was stamped on in a league game at Reading and although I was in a lot of pain initially, I never thought it would take almost a year to recover from. My recovering was not helped by Watford's new club physio, a guy called Jav Mugal. In all honesty, he messed me about. He knew that he was only temporary and was leaving the club that summer and although it would be wrong for me to say that he didn't care, he just didn't seem to be that bothered about finding what the root of my problem was.

My right-foot instep was causing me considerable pain by now and when our new physio Phil Edwards came in, I thought things would be sorted straightaway. I was told to go away for the summer to rest but by the time I came back for pre-season, the pain was still agonising when I kicked a ball. Phil was trying all sorts of treatments, but they had little effect. I was a worried man. 'If the club physio doesn't have a clue what's the matter with me, what hope do I have?' were the words which kept going through my mind. I was in deep depression. I was tired of trying all these different treatments to no avail and I started going out and drinking quite heavily. It was now a good six months since that Reading game and I thought my career could well be over before it had really begun.

There was only one option left for me, an operation to discover if there was any internal damage. As it happens, when the surgeons opened me up they found the problem straight away – the capsule ligaments in my foot had pulled away from the bone leaving a hole, which was causing all the pain. Relief was followed by frustration as my recovery would then take another five months.

Not only that, the task of turning our season around proved to be too much for Taylor and relegation to Division Two was inevitable. Could it get any lower for me? To be honest, I didn't go to too many games in the latter stages of that season. It was too painful to watch, knowing that I should have been out there, helping the boys. To their credit, they put together a great little run but it was too little, too late. The day we got relegated, I remember sitting at home with my feet up and saw the scoreline come through on teletext.

So it was now in Division Two where I would be plying my trade. I returned to action in late February of that season and after one reserve run-out, I was back in the squad and made the bench for our trip to Brentford. I got a great reception from our wonderful band of supporters and I felt great to be back. I then went on to score four goals in my next two games and my rollercoaster ride had now reached another peak. But I was soon hitting another trough. The Second Division is no place for the faint-hearted. This league, with all due respect, was full of cloggers at that time and for a player who had been out of action for the best part of a year, I was struggling. I was struggling both physically and mentally and what followed was the most barren run of my football career – 12 games without a goal – and the frustration was setting in.

Things came to a head at Wrexham. I received my marching orders for the first time in my career for a terrible over-the-top tackle and was rightly slated by the management in the dressing room after the game. We lost 2–0 and they thought I'd cost them the game. That was the lowest point of my career. I was then dropped for two or three games and I think Graham was also disappointed in me for turning down a new contract which he offered me on transfer deadline day that March. I was out of contract in the summer and wanted to wait until then to explore all my options. In any case, the contract they offered me was not what I wanted. I had to think of my future. The atmosphere turned frosty to say the least.

It was at this point that I had also heard of interest from Ipswich Town. My Watford team-mate Steve Palmer was a former Town player and still kept in contact with the club and their manager George Burley. He informed me that they were interested in signing me, so I also wanted to hear from them. There was no way I was going to plunge straight in and sign on the dotted line for Watford. I don't think anyone, in any walk of life, would have done that. You owe it to yourself to at least listen to offers in these situations.

By now I'd also employed the agent Phil Smith to look after my financial matters and when I met again with Watford during the summer, the offer on the table was still not what I was looking for. I felt they were trying to pull a fast one – and it was promptly rejected. I was not asking for silly money, just security, but it wasn't going to happen. I felt I was worth more and that was when I knew I had to leave Vicarage Road.

Port Vale boss John Rudge had also come in for me at this point, as he was looking to replace Tony Naylor, but I had my heart set on Ipswich, a club which is renowned for its good football and an established First Division team which I thought I could do a job for.

I travelled down to Suffolk to meet Burley, the chairman David Sheepshanks and have a look around Portman Road. I was mightily impressed and things were looking good. The contract on the table was far better than Watford had offered. Not only that, I could travel to the ground in just over an hour from my Stevenage home, so everything looked perfect.

I went home to think over a few things, but in my mind I was already an Ipswich player. All that stood in the way was the transfer fee, and I envisaged no problems.

So it was to my dismay that the deal fell through over a paltry £50,000. Ipswich were offering £300,000 but Watford would not budge on the £350,000 fee they'd put on my head, so it looked as if the transfer deal would go to a tribunal.

But having delved a little deeper, Ipswich were already going down that route with Mark Venus, the big centre half from Wolves. And Football League rules stipulate that you can only sign one player at a time through a tribunal. Regrettably, they pulled out of the deal and I was left devastated and, more importantly, in no-man's land.

So it was back to pre-season training with Watford. I wanted to move on and Taylor knew that, but we all just got on with things. Although it was hard to get motivated, I knew I had to get fit, so I put in plenty of effort in training. Whether I was playing at Watford that season or somewhere else, I would be no use unless I was at the peak of my fitness.

In the meantime a new club had come from nowhere into the equation. It was Sunderland, newly relegated to Division One after a terrible Premiership campaign. It was after my final visit to George Burley in a last-ditch effort to save my transfer that I discovered their manager, Peter Reid, had shown an interest. My agent told me the news as I sat, devastated, in the front of his car at

Portman Road. I didn't believe him at first so he gave Peter a call from inside his car on the hands-free phone. Peter didn't know I was in the car at the time but I heard those comforting words 'Yeah, I rate Kevin Phillips and I'm definitely interested'.

Reid, a legend for Everton and England, respected me as a player. I don't think there can be a greater compliment towards me. From that moment on I wanted to be a Sunderland player but there were plenty of things to consider. After all, I knew Sunderland was some distance from Stevenage. And that was all I knew. I didn't have much of a clue about the team, the stadium or the implications the move would have on my life. It would mean uprooting my family and, in particular, my fiancée Julie who was carrying our first child at the time.

I'd moved to Southampton, but this was different. This was permanent. But after Julie and I sat down and discussed the matter, we knew we wouldn't be moving away for ever and if it was in the best interests of my career, then I should do it. So I took the gamble and without even having a preliminary round of talks, I was on my way to sign. I knew Sunderland were a massive club just by talking to family and friends, and it was probably Glenn Roeder who swung the decision for me.

'Kevin,' he said. 'I spent six years in the north east with Newcastle and they were the happiest days of my life. If you are a success in that neck of the woods, the fans will love you. You will become a legend.'

That was good enough for me and before you could say 'signing on fee', I was on my way up the A1.

Saying goodbye was not easy. Not just to Julie and my

mother – whom I would not see for some time – but to my Watford team-mates and staff. We had a good team spirit and I had some great times at the club. Watford FC will always remain close to my heart because they gave me my big break and I'll be eternally grateful to them. It was also sad to leave behind the fans – the ones who started off the now infamous 'Super Kevin Phillips' chant. It was a song I was not too keen on at first, but one which I've grown to love. When they look back at what I did, I'm sure they'll agree that I paid back my transfer fee and only moved on because I wanted to better myself. The money was not right at Watford, but then I was also given a chance to play at a higher level. I think most Hornets fans could see that and I didn't receive any animosity from them when I walked out of Vicarage Road for the final time.

I still keep in contact with a few of their players to this day – skipper Robert Page in particular – and in Graham Taylor, they have a manager who is up there with the best when it comes to club management and I'm sure that he will take the club to even greater heights.

It's incredible to think that within the space of just over a year, they've gone from Second Division champions to Premiership hopefuls. I was hoping to be at Wembley for their play-off final against Bolton but although I was injured at the time, Kevin Keegan asked me to be part of the squad for the Euro 2000 qualifier with Sweden, so I couldn't make it. You cannot turn down a call from the England boss, no matter what the circumstances, but I watched the entire game on TV and was jumping around the room when Watford won the game.

It was a wonderful moment to see the club take their place among the elite last season, although it was probably inevitable that they would last only one season in the top-flight. They had come from Division Two to the Premiership in consecutive seasons and this was too much, too soon for a club of their stature. Thankfully, they did not suffer the indignity of a season of heavy defeats, and I'm sure they will come back stronger for the experience.

Taylor's magic has rubbed off on his Watford players again and they've proved they haven't needed me. Graham's got a settled side now and a few new faces from when I left the club. But I left at the right time. It was time for a new adventure, a new life and the opening chapter of a period in my life which I think I'll be hard-pressed to ever beat.

CHAPTER TWO

The Making of a Mackem

By all accounts, it was Glenn Roeder, again, who had a massive say in my next footballing adventure. Apparently, Peter Reid had been tracking my Watford colleague David Connelly, who eventually took advantage of his freedom of contract in return for a substantial pay packet and signing-on fee at Feyenoord in Holland.

Glenn had discovered this after sitting next to Sunderland coach Alan Durban at a sportsmens' dinner in the north east. He somehow managed to persuade Alan that I was the man they should be looking at, not David, if they wanted an immediate return for their transfer fee.

But whenever I ask Peter why he went for me, he insists that I stuck in his mind after we drew 1–1 at Roker Park in a league game in my first year. Apparently I was causing his defence a host of problems and pulling them out of position. He says I looked lively that day and he'd never forgotten about me. Never knew I'd made such an impression!

Whatever the true story is – and maybe it's a combination of the two – I was just delighted to be heading up to Wearside to be joining one of the biggest clubs in Britain, even if I didn't know it at the time.

Thankfully this time there were no transfer hitches. Everything was in place for me. My agent had already been to see Peter to set up the financial package and the contract they laid on the table was even better than the one at Ipswich. That's when I knew that they were deadly serious about me and had money to show that they were moving in the right direction.

The two clubs were also happy with the transfer fee this time. I would cost Sunderland £350,000, rising to £650,000 on appearances and promotion. So after all their haggling Watford were happy, and they must be bloody delighted with the way things have turned out since. They've certainly had their money's worth out of a £10,000 signing from non-league Baldock Town!

As the days passed and in the week leading up to me signing for Sunderland, it was gradually starting to sink in that this was a huge club and I was going to be a big signing. Peter phoned me at home after the fee had been agreed and I remember his words vividly to this day.

'Kevin,' he said. 'I want you to score me the goals to get us back into the Premiership.'

I told him that I wouldn't let him down but at this stage I thought I was just going as a squad member, and that the club would be in the market for an established striker to *really* score them the goals to get them back in the top flight. After all, the fans were crying out for a proven centre-forward. Their top scorer the previous season was Paul Stewart and I think he only got four or five league goals. A terrible return, and you can hardly blame the fans for wanting a lot more.

Just as the car was loaded for the long trek north to put pen to paper, the *Sunderland Echo* had tracked me down and were wanting to know how I felt about the move and playing for Peter Reid. Blimey, I was big-time news for the first time in my life. I thought I was just a low-key signing and at the time I probably was. But this was news in Sunderland and it really hit home that this was a massive club, where any news is going to be big news.

Anyway, the trusty old Astra was packed and I was out on the road at 5.00 am. I'd been told by my brother-in-law Barry that the trip would take about three-and-a-half hours. That's how naive I was with regards to Sunderland and the north east in general. I hadn't a clue where the place was and the thought of travelling so far almost gave me a nosebleed!

But I was alone and as I got closer, the adrenalin was rushing around my body. With the help of my battered old atlas, I arrived at 9.00 am but I hadn't a clue where the stadium was.

I pulled into a garage next to the Board Inn (one of our pick-up points for away games) and when I asked for directions, the bloke said, 'New stadium or old?' I just presumed Peter would be at the new stadium, so I followed the directions and then, on the horizon, the stadium emerged out of the sky.

'Jesus Christ, it's massive!' I yelled as the blood began to race around my body. I'd heard that Sunderland were building a new stadium but this was bloody incredible. This stadium was up there with the best in Britain, if not Europe and it was far too good to be hosting First Division football.

I got out of my car with this huge bowl-like structure leering over me and asked one of the builders where Peter Reid's office was. 'At Roker Park' was the response. Apparently the Sunderland staff were still based at the old ground until everything was in place for the grand opening later that summer. So, after asking for more directions, I found Roker Park, not quite as imposing but still a nice stadium all the same.

As I walked into the reception, I admit that I was fretting with nerves. The time had come to meet Peter face to face for the first time. What mood would he be in? Would he put the fear of God into me? It was like going back to school and facing the headmaster after you'd been in trouble. I walked up the stairs, knocked on the door and entered. Peter was sitting at his desk, with feet on table, drinking a cup of tea. His mannerisms put me at ease straightaway and he welcomed me to Sunderland.

Also present were Alan Durban and Paul Bracewell and they all made me feel welcome from the start. No longer was I back at school, or facing a job interview. I was among friends and I could start to breathe a little easier.

After a brief chat about the club and his plans for their first season back in Division One, Peter took me in his car to the club's training ground to meet the players. But as we turned out of Roker Park, we drove along the seafront. 'Blimey,' I said to him. 'I didn't even know Sunderland was by the sea!' It was also a warm, sunny day and there were kids playing on the beach. It was a lovely sight and I felt I wanted to stay. I'd always wanted to live close to the sea.

As we pulled up at the training ground gates, we were greeted by 50 or so fans who rushed over towards the car, wanting Peter's autograph. I couldn't believe it. They'd all come to watch the team train, which was a far cry from my days at Watford when we got one man and his dog, when the dog could be bothered!

I watched the players train and although I didn't recognise many of them, there were a few familiar faces among the lads being put through their pre-season paces. The most striking was big Niall Quinn. He's always going to stand out among the crowd wherever he is, but I paid particular attention to him because he was another player I used to go and watch as a fan at Arsenal. I found it hard to take in at that stage that I might just be playing alongside him within a few weeks.

Another player whom I instantly recognised was Lee Clark. He'd attracted big headlines following his £2.5 million move from deadly rivals Newcastle. He was major news, having made such a shock transfer and I realised just how big a shock it was as the weeks went on, and I got a better feel for the intense rivalry between both sets of supporters.

I'd also seen Mickey Gray play on the TV and, to be honest, I was in awe of the entire situation. The stadium, the management, the players – it was a world away from what I'd been used to. It was hard to take it all in.

Talking of the stadium, Peter took me inside for a look around. It was far from complete at this stage but the pitch had been laid and the seats were starting to go in. I walked out to the centre-circle and looked around at this vast bowl which was to house 42,000 manic Mackem fans. I thought Vicarage Road was a nice ground but this was unbelievable. I just kept imagining what it would be like to score a goal and hear the crowd roar.

But it didn't finish there. I had to go through the traumas of a medical for the first time, back at Roker, with our physio Neil Metcalfe. It seemed to take an eternity as everything was checked, from my ears to my ankles. Then it was off to the Washington Hospital for scans on my ankles, knees and hips. Having seen Ipswich pull out at the last minute, I was concerned that my foot injury would show up and that I'd be sent packing down the A1 again. I'd seen too much to want to go home and I was praying that everything would be okay.

Some swelling did show up on the scans but not enough to warrant a rejection. I got the green light to sign. At last, I was a Sunderland player.

I got back to my hotel, the Washington Moat House, at 5.00 pm and just crashed out onto my bed. I looked up to the ceiling, but I still had a couple of niggling doubts as to whether I'd done the right thing. This was a big club, a very big club as I'd quickly discovered but was I big enough to be on the payroll? Then I spoke to Julie and she was delighted with the way things had gone. That put me at ease and as I turned in for the night I just said to myself 'Sod it, let's go for it!' and I haven't looked back since.

It was time to impress. Day Two saw me hit the training ground for the first time. First impressions last and it was just my luck to have a bit of a 'mare when it came to shooting practice. 'How much?!' were the cries from behind me as I shanked a couple well wide of the target. It was all in good spirit; well, at least I hope it was!

I found the training very enjoyable, and not so regimented as it was under Taylor at Watford – and this was only pre-season. But in general, training at Sunderland is better than anything I've experienced before. A typical training session at Sunderland for the first three months of the season sees us work from 10.30 to 1.00 pm, or an 11.00 am start for Niall Quinn as he's always late! Coach Bobby Saxton and the gaffer will vary the sessions to include plenty of keep ball, five-a-sides, then finish off with some hard running and shooting. Later in the week we'll work on set pieces as the weekend game looms. But by Christmas, with the games coming thick and fast, training eases right down and it's not unusual for us to be back inside within an hour. We are already fit, it's just a case of ticking over, although I'll always stay behind to work on my shooting.

After my first session, it was off to Ireland for our pre-season tour the following day. And having lived in the pockets of my team-mates for five days, I would soon become one of the lads.

I was also helped by having Quinny as a room mate, the legend I admired so much as a fan. The first thing I said when I phoned home was 'I'm sharing a room with

Niall Quinn!' but obviously I waited until the big man had left the room!

I was nervous being in the same room as him, to be honest. I didn't know what to say to him. He was a top-rate international who even Alan Shearer calls 'Legend'.

But he soon put me at ease. 'Just enjoy the experience,' he said to me. 'You are at a big club now, but just do your best'. I soon discovered he was a genuinely nice guy. He was a big help to me in those early days and has remained so to this day.

We played a local side in Dublin the following evening and I was pitched straight in with Quinny. I didn't manage to get on the scoresheet, but the two of us linked up really well and the rest of the lads were soon patting me on the back – they knew then that I was a good player and would fit in well.

We went on to play two more games in Dublin, and I played in one-and-a-half of them, but I was getting strong vibes from the management and the teams being picked that I would be involved in our first league game of the season at Sheffield United. Maybe Peter Reid was right, maybe I really was the man he wanted to score the goals to get the club back into the Premiership.

I was also mixing more with the lads now. At the meal table, I was no longer the lad on the end with his head bowed. I was joining in with the banter. I was also helped by the fact that Jody Craddock and Chris Byrne were also staying in the Washington Moat House Hotel at the same time as me. For the first few weeks, the three of us did everything together. We were the new boys.

Back in England, we had two more friendlies, at

Carlisle United, which we won 1–0 and where I came on as a sub, and then a trip to new-boys Macclesfield, in which I scored my first goal for the club and we won by the same scoreline.

It was at this point that I'd got my first taste of the wonderful support Sunderland attracts. These were low key friendlies against, with all respect, lower division sides. But we were bringing 600 fans with us to these games – we even had 200 or so watching us in Dublin, but I'm sure that had something to do with the ale and the nightlife!

To see so many at these games was an incredible sight and they got behind me from the start. Julie sat in with the fans for the Carlisle game and she came out stunned after all the noise they created. It was her first Sunderland game and like me, she couldn't believe their passion and commitment. 'Bit different to Vicarage Road!' was her response.

It was good to see Julie again and it was hard knowing that she would soon be back on her way home, leaving me in the hotel. We took some time out to look at a few houses while she was up and we'd found a place we liked in Brancepeth. We jumped into the deal, to be honest, without looking at all the options because I just wanted to get settled and get her up here with me. Although it can be fun living in a hotel for the first few nights, it soon gets boring and there are only so many toasted sandwiches you can order on room service. Luckily, we had a golf course next to the hotel where I was staying and that helped pass the time away. Whenever I'm not playing football, I love a round of golf, it's a great way to get away from the pressures which the game brings. But I couldn't spend every passing hour on the course. I was getting bored holed up in my room. It was getting to the point where I felt like a prisoner. The move just couldn't come quick enough for me.

But on the pitch, everything was now falling into place and Peter was delighted with my progress. 'Just keep going and do the same things you were good at at Watford,' he said. 'You're a good player, but you're on a much bigger stage now. If you just be yourself, you'll be fine.' Which, in my eyes, was translated as 'you're in the team.'

So the boss was happy, the fans had seen a glimpse of what I could do but I still had to win over the local press. As a footballer, the press can make or break you, no matter what league or what standard of football you are playing, and they were still waiting for the manager to sign a top-class player. One of the local papers ran a headline 'WHO'S KEVIN PHILLIPS? If you have any idea, can you please phone up and let us know'.

They were expecting a multi-million pound arrival. This would go on for another three months and it was up to me to prove that I *was* the star signing. I might have been cheap, but I had the platform and the ability to show that I could become the bargain buy of the season. Determination was again the all-important word, all I needed was a good start to the season.

But before I could start thinking of Bramall Lane and scoring on my league debut, I was suddenly wracked with guilt and fraught with worry.

'Shit, I'm suspended, I can't play!' I said to myself as I

drove back from training just a week or so before the season's start. It had dawned on me that I was carrying over a one-match ban for my sending off at the end of the previous season for Watford.

But how would I tell Peter? I'm about to ruin all his preparation work. How could I have been so stupid? One thing's for sure, he's not going to be happy and I'm certainly not going to be flavour of the month with him. The new boy's in trouble already.

Peter received the news from my agent and, just as I thought, he wasn't happy. It was time for my first run-in with the gaffer. 'What's the matter with you, why didn't you tell me?' were the first words he said when we met up the following day. I was uneasy already, now I felt really uncomfortable.

But to Peter's credit, he's not the kind of person, let alone manager, who holds a grudge and he knew that I had made a genuine mistake. Thankfully, once the dust had settled a little bit, he had a laugh and joke about it with me. But I couldn't help but think that I had blown my big chance. If the team gets off to a good start, then I'm well out of the picture.

Our final warm-up game was the big one. The mighty Ajax were the visitors to celebrate the official opening of our Stadium of Light. With the start of the season just days away, I wasn't expecting to play due to my forthcoming suspension but the manager opted to start with me and it was then that I really did feel a part of his plans. I felt wanted and I felt rated. If Peter Reid believes in me then I must surely believe in myself. From that moment on, I knew I was the main man.

The game, indeed the entire spectacle, is something that will live with me for the rest of my life. Our skipper Kevin Ball warned me to get to the ground at least three hours before kick-off because the streets would be pandemonium. I thought he was winding me up at first, but when Kevin is serious, you know it, so I took notice of what he said and set out at four o'clock, giving myself plenty of time to arrive.

To be honest, I wasn't a big fan of Bally's in my early days at Sunderland. I quickly found out that he was the hard man of the team and he trains just like he plays. I'd say it to his face now but when I first arrived at the club, I didn't like him. He was too serious, too hyped up and he seemed like someone I just couldn't relate to.

I remember in those early weeks, when I had just started doing well and scoring goals, that he came in for a challenge and caught me right down the shin. Now most players wear moulded studs for training but not Bally. No, he has to wear six inch metal studs and he raked all the skin off my leg. I limped off, pissed off, and fortunate not to have done anything more serious.

To get my own back, I wrapped my leg in bandages and when he came off at the end, I said I would be out of action for weeks. With this he was really apologetic – until we told him the truth!

But I must admit that I grew to like Kevin a lot. He seemed to relax much more towards the end of his spell at the club and once I got to know him, I quickly found out that he would do anything for you.

It's just that Bally's a winner. He never settles for second best, regardless of the situation he's in. He's been sent off in training plenty of times and he even squared up to Bobby Saxton last season. He just hates losing, even head tennis, and every team needs someone like him.

Kevin will always be known as Mr Sunderland. He knows the club inside out and true to his word, he was spot on with his prediction. As I approached the stadium from my hotel, the roads were a sea of red and white, and it reminded me of FA Cup final day at Wembley. It took me a full 45 minutes to make a journey which usually takes about a third of that time.

The atmosphere outside the ground was electric, a carnival atmosphere to herald the dawning of a new era for Sunderland. It was the start of a new period in my life too, but I wouldn't be able to celebrate until I'd got my first outing in a Sunderland shirt out of the way. And in any case, I was too nervous at this point to join in with the fun.

The build up to the game was phenomenal and I can remember standing on the side of the pitch with Status Quo blaring out all their old hits from the centre circle. The crowd were up on their feet and the noise was unbearable. I was standing next to Quinny and he said, 'Take in the noise, it doesn't get much better than this'. To which I responded, 'You what? The stadium's not even full yet!'

Then it was back down to the changing room for the real business to get underway. The adrenalin was taking over, but I was still a bag of nerves. Sky Television were covering the game live, we were up against one of the strongest sides in world football, it was my debut and I knew I would be judged from the moment I stepped out onto the lush grass. I think I had a good enough reason to have the odd butterfly in my stomach.

And if I wasn't worried enough, one of the lads in the dressing room said to me, 'This is your chance, Kev. There are 42,000 fans out there and you don't want to get on the wrong side of them. Sunderland fans either love you or hate you, there's no middle ground. Just make sure you come off the pitch on their side.'

Brilliant. As if I didn't have enough pressure heaped on my shoulders. Talk about words of encouragement!

But in a funny way, I used those words to my advantage. I thought, 'Well, the fans are expecting us to sign a big name, so if I did well, then that will be brilliant, but if I didn't have the best of games, it wouldn't be the end of the world.' I was doing all I could to take the heat out of the situation.

As I walked down that tunnel for the first time, I couldn't believe the noise. To start with, the classical music of Prokofiev boomed down the sound system, before we entered the pitch to the sound of Republica. It was phenomenal and the fans greeted us in true ticker-tape fashion. It was the biggest game of my life and it was only a friendly. Goodness knows what they'd be like if we had a real crunch game to play later in the season.

Just as we lined up to kick-off, my heart was pumping. I was hoping Ajax would rotate their players and use it as a real warm-up. No such luck. As soon as I moved up the field I had that old campaigner Danny Blind watching my every move. As if I didn't have enough on my plate.

What pleased me more than anything was that, like at Watford, Sunderland try to play good football but could mix it up with a few longer balls to the big target man up front. This helped me settle down very quickly and, just as at Watford with the likes of Wilkinson and Dixon, I hit it off immediately with big Niall. I was feeding off of him throughout the first half and I made sure that I looked busy, so that the fans would notice me. I thought I was doing okay, although I did give a few balls away; overall, the performance was steady.

In all honesty, it was a game played at a slow pace, with management and players alike knowing that the last thing they needed was a serious injury with the big kick-off just days away. With that Sheffield United game in mind, I knew that I would be substituted as the gaffer wanted to look at the side he would play that day, so it was no surprise when the number ten card was lifted up. But this was already a critical period in my Sunderland career. How would the fans react? With boos or cheers? I was worried but I shouldn't have been. I received a standing ovation. I knew it would still take time but I felt as if I was one of them. I felt I had been transformed into a Mackem at that precise moment.

Not that the press all saw it that way. The game finished 0–0 and the words 'Striker Required' were still making headlines. Come on, give me a chance!

Anyway, I came off the pitch feeling happy with my contribution and headed straight down the tunnel for a well earned shower. But after my gaff over the Sheffield United game, I was soon dropping clanger number two. Just as I was putting my foot on a pipe to clean my leg, the pipe broke and water went gushing everywhere. The stadium's just minutes old and I'm creating mayhem already. But even worse, the water was now flooding into the main part of the dressing room where the players had left their clothes. Thankfully, I managed to attract the attention of a steward and a couple of the trainees managed to mop up the mess before any of the first-teamers had a chance to see what had happened. A catastrophe had been avoided. I had saved myself from earning the nickname 'Frank Spencer' and, more importantly, I saved myself another confrontation with the gaffer. What would he have thought if I'd soaked his legendary designer gear!

The following morning I spoke to Robert Page and, having watched the game on TV, he admitted to feeling just a little bit envious of the paths the two of us were taking. He was preparing for another season of football in Division Two, whereas I was playing for a quality team in an amazing stadium. I'd made the right decision.

It was then on to the Sheffield United game, a massive fixture for Sunderland in their bid to bounce straight back into the top-flight. With myself on the sidelines, Quinny played on his own in attack, as we put five men in midfield. It turned out to be a disastrous game for us, as we lost 2–0. We were roundly beaten and looked like we were struggling to adapt to the pace of Division One football.

In the dressing room after the game, Peter had gone absolutely mad. 'You lot didn't want it as much as them,' he said, although the language was far stronger. 'It's not going to be easy and you've got to work much harder if you're going to get out of this league.'

The season was just a day old and the heads were down and the knives were out. The local, and national press come to think of it, had a field day. The atmosphere surrounding the team and the club was totally negative. Blimey, we've only played one game and already we're a beaten side in some people's eyes. But that's the pressures which come with a big club. Results have to be instant, you can't live for tomorrow and I was learning quickly.

On a personal level, the day at Bramall Lane was obviously filled with mixed emotions. Of course I was gutted that we'd lost the game but sitting up in the stands, I was just pleased that nobody had come in and stolen my thunder. No-one more than me would have been happier to see us score goals and win, but in a funny way I was glad that the strikers hadn't made their mark. I think that's only natural for any player sitting on the sidelines. I think every footballer's the same. It left the door wide open for me in the next game, at home to Man City. I had a chance and I had to grab it with both hands.

The 1997/98 season was just five days old and already it felt as if the next game was critical for our promotion hopes. We simply had to win. A full house, live TV cameras and strong opposition. I wasn't surprised to be included in the starting line-up this time.

I just knew I had to score; having drawn a blank in my first game against Ajax, nothing else would be good enough. It was a big enough occasion already and there's me heaping more pressure on myself. But that's just the way I am. Three prolific seasons later and I'm still doing exactly the same. I'm too hard on myself but if I haven't scored, it's the end of the world for me and I'm already aching to put it right in the next game.

My Mum and Julie came up for the game and I wanted to do well for them, too. We travelled to the game together and, just like the Ajax match, the stadium was jam-packed. The kick-off was delayed by 15 minutes to get all the fans in and the mood in the dressing room was calm and collected. There was no finger pointing. Everybody knew what they had to do. We had to get a win at all costs.

Again I linked up well with Quinny who, when it comes to the crunch, you can always count on to put in a top-class performance. It was no surprise then when he slotted home the opener and the stadium erupted. I was caught up in the euphoria too. Here I was, playing for a massive club like Sunderland, partnering Niall Quinn and playing in front of the loudest fans I'd ever heard in an amazing setting for a football match. I just lost it and went mad, jumping on Quinny and clenching my fists in the direction of the crowd.

Again, I wanted to put in a 'busy' performance so, just in case I didn't score, I looked as if I was fighting hard for the cause. I'd already been up-ended once by City's big defender Tony Vaughan early in the game and then later on, he took me out again and was shown the red card.

The crowd were on their feet, applauding me. They had clearly taken to me and I just wanted to top it off with a goal. But that was looking unlikely when their Georgian wizard Georgi Kinkladze provided a moment of magic, cutting through our side like butter before being upended in the box and finishing with a top class penalty.

It was back to 1–1, there were 15 minutes left on the clock and the crowd was getting anxious. One point from a possible six would have been a terrible return. We just couldn't afford to let that happen.

Then, my date with destiny arrived. Mickey Gray swung over a free-kick from just inside City's half, the ball was flicked on to Kevin Ball and as his volley was pushed out by their keeper, I was on hand to smash the ball into the back of the net.

GOAL! I'd done it, I'd given myself, the crowd, the management and the press the perfect tonic. I'd scored on my debut and put us back on the winning way.

It was a fantastic feeling, one of the greatest I'll ever experience and I celebrated, Klinsmann-style, with a full length dive towards the nearest corner flag.

After being mobbed, I ran back to the centre circle and it felt as if a massive weight had been lifted off my shoulders. I knew that I should be starting the next game and I could just get on with the business of scoring goals – just what Peter Reid wanted from me.

We had another couple of chances to make the game safe and just as the referee was about to blow the whistle, I teed up Lee Clark for his first goal for the club. Cue crowd eruptions once more with the goal and the final whistle.

Everyone received a pat on the back from the gaffer after the game and I was just delighted to return the faith that he had shown in me. Still need a new striker do we? I didn't think so, and even the press were starting to have second thoughts as all the reports on my performance were really positive. I don't think they could have written anything else.

Everything went right for me, the shower didn't break and the press were swarming round me after the game. It seemed to take forever to get out of the stadium and then I had to deal with fans asking for my autograph as I approached my car. At this stage, quite a few of them were getting me mixed up with Lee Clark but that didn't last too long, thank goodness. He's far uglier than me! But it was nice to be the centre of attention all the same. Being in the spotlight was something I'd dreamed about as a kid and now I was living that dream. And it's true, in those early weeks it was like a fantasy. Although I was playing in Division One, I felt that with the quality we had in the side and with the support we had, we were Premiership-class in everything but name. The difficult bit would prove to be getting there.

I was buzzing as I got in the car. I think Julie and my Mum were still trying to come to terms with what they'd witnessed. This was big time. It was a Friday night, I had the weekend to myself, and could easily have spent it celebrating in the north-east, my new home.

But it was back down the A1 for me, to be back with the rest of my family and friends, some of whom I hadn't seen since I'd set out for that initial trip to Sunderland a few weeks earlier. I was eager to get home and maybe the adrenalin in my body was the reason why I was nicked for speeding that evening. I would have been gutted to receive three points on my license any other day, but nothing was going to spoil my evening. I was now a Sunderland player and a Sunderland goalscorer at that. I didn't have to prove anything to anybody anymore.

CHAPTER THREE

The Good, the Bad and the Ugly

I have the utmost respect for Peter Reid. In my eyes he is the ultimate players' manager, a great motivator and a man you can approach if you have a problem. Our tremendous desire and will to win stems from him. He is a winner. Hard but fair. And the players respond to that.

He is not, however, a man you should get on the wrong side of. Do that, and you run the risk of throwing your chances in his side right down the drain. And as everyone saw in *Premier Passions*, the fly-on-the-wall television documentary about Sunderland AFC, he has a fierce, almost scary temper at times if we are not doing the business on the park.

In the three seasons I have been at Sunderland, there hasn't been too many occasions when he's had to fly off the handle but at Vale Park, the week after the Man City game, he erupted, and how!

Having comfortably disposed of City, the confidence in the camp was high. The aim was to put together a good early run, get ourselves into the promotion frame and hopefully put pressure on the teams around us. That season I thought Wolves, Birmingham, Nottingham Forest, Ipswich and Middlesbrough would be our main challengers. I did not think Port Vale would prove to be such an obstacle.

In all honesty, we thought we would walk it. The attitude just wasn't right. Within a minute, we were 1–0 down but if that was the kick up the backside we needed, the response was pathetic. We just couldn't raise our game and went further behind. We were waiting for the referee to blow his half-time whistle and the game was already over as a spectacle. It was 2–0. Embarrassing. We had let ourselves down, the management and the incredible 1,000 fans who had made the long trek to Vale Park for a midweek match. They were booing us long and loud – and rightly so. I just wanted to rewind the clock 45 minutes and start again.

My own conscience was cleared ever so slightly after scoring a consolation goal just before the break. I thought I'd done my bit. I couldn't have been more wrong.

After we'd sloped off to the dressing room 0–3 behind, we all sat down, the door was slammed and Peter let rip. He was in a rage – and rightly so – but I'd never experienced anything like it before.

A tray of tea was sitting on a table in the corner of the room, but not for long! In his rage, the gaffer launched the whole lot into the air and straight out of the window.

All you could hear were the screams of people walking past outside, being attacking by scalding PG Tips!

When you think back, it was quite a comical moment but it was no laughing matter at the time. Everyone had their heads down and Peter then went on to slaughter each and every one of us, picking us off one at a time. 'You're shit... You're crap... Was it worth you f***ing turning up...' Then it was my turn. Having scored, I thought I would escape lightly. 'And you, you're a good player but I think you're a homer. I only think you can fucking play at home.'

What? I'd only played two games in the Stadium of Light and this was my first away game for the club. How could he judge me on that? I was gutted. I felt really down that he felt that way, although in hindsight, he probably said it out of frustration. But, the best way for me to respond was on the pitch. I had to let my feet do the talking.

The second half display was much better. The players had responded to the roasting but the deficit was too much to pull back and we lost 3–1. We just had to put it down to a bad day at the office and make sure we put things right in the next match at home to Norwich. I should be alright, we're playing at home after all!

Now you know when things are not going your way when you totally outplay a team for 90 minutes and are then hit by a sucker punch in the closing stages of the game. That's exactly what happened to us against The Canaries. This was one of the most one-sided games I've ever played in and just when we're throwing men forward to try and get all three points, Norwich defender

Daryl Sutch somehow breaks through to put the ball under Lionel Perez.

Cue celebrations for the small band of visiting supporters, cue a chorus of boos from the other 38,000 or so fans. I just couldn't believe what was happening, especially as I'd hit the post and the crossbar. I had walked into a bad dream. This just wasn't meant to be happening. When I signed, everything was hunky dory. Now it's fast turning into a nightmare. Okay, I had scored two goals but I doubt many people cared at this stage. Walking off the pitch was incredible, like something you see in those continental matches on TV. Our own fans were spitting at us, objects were being chucked and the gaffer was getting some right abuse. It was a sorry time for everyone and after the incident, the club erected a canopy for players, just in case there was similar abuse in the future.

The gaffer again went pretty mad. It was 'Fuck' this and 'Bollocks' that, but although he was probably frustrated, no-one would dare say that he was wrong and that we were unlucky. Never in my time at Sunderland has anyone back-chatted the gaffer when he's been full into a rage. It would take a brave person, and a silly one at that. Plus, we've got too much respect for a man with such a good track record in football management.

'There's nothing we can do about it now,' he said as he walked out of the room. 'But we're running out of lives. We've got to start winning, otherwise we can kiss goodbye to the lot.'

We were down, and so were the fans. They have

turned out to be brilliant towards me and the team since then, but at that stage I was disappointed in them. I know they pay their money and they deserve their say. But I just felt they should have got behind us a bit more during this rocky period. It's an old cliché but when you've got the crowd behind you, it really does feel like you've got an extra player.

I don't think the new stadium was helping us at this point either. When you looked at our opponents during the warm-ups, you could see in their eyes that this was like a cup final to them. It's probably the biggest and best set-up many of them would play in all season and they wanted to make the most of it.

On a personal level, I wasn't being helped by being holed up in my hotel room during this opening month of the campaign. You've got far too much time on your hands, doing absolutely nothing. I had nothing to occupy my mind, except thinking about Sunderland and where things were going wrong.

But there was the odd bright moment, like the time when Chris Byrne completely lost the plot in the hotel bar. We had only just sat down one night to watch the football on the TV and we were drinking coffee as we had a big game later in the week. Chris was flanked by me and Jody Craddock and we were all sitting on these high stools at the bar.

Later in the game, Chris had ordered another coffee and just as he's got up off his seat to pay his money, Jody's pulled his stool away without him noticing. Well, he's gone to sit back, with cup in hand, and gone crashing to the floor, which was some fall.

We were in absolute stitches, I had tears in my eyes, but Chris didn't see the funny side at all.

He went mad, and squared up to the two of us. We thought he'd just dust himself down and get on with watching the game, but he was serious. He really wanted to take the two of us on. 'Where I come from, you just don't fucking do things like that,' he said in his strong Mancunian accent. 'You need a fucking good seeing to.'

Somehow we calmed him down but it took some time and at one stage he was ready to take the barman on as well. You never really could get the Mancunian out of him and at one time he went AWOL in Manchester and the gaffer had to go and find him. It wasn't long before he was sold to Macclesfield, which is a great shame because the manager really rated him. He was a good player.

But such incidents were few and far between at the hotel and, thankfully, I moved into the house in Brancepeth in September, then Julie joined me. I was occupied by sorting the house out the way we wanted it and at last, I felt secure and settled in the area and had someone to talk to. It was as if another huge weight had been lifted from me. Now I could just get on with my football.

It was no surprise that I then went on to hit a bit of a purple patch, scoring twice in back-to-back wins against Oxford and at Bradford. The team had found its feet at last and we were starting to gel. We won both games and all of a sudden the mood had brightened over the city.

In fact, the win against Bradford was one of our best all season. We were 4–0 up at half time and playing some delightful football. I was also very pleased with my goal. I managed to cut inside a couple of defenders before drilling a low left-foot shot past their keeper. I had now scored four goals in five starts for the club and had already beaten Paul Stewart's tally of league goals for the whole of the previous season!

People were finally starting to sit up and take notice of this Kevin Phillips character. I had won the fans over at this stage, no question, and the press were now completely behind me. I was getting more phone calls for more interviews and getting stopped in the street a lot more. People wanted to talk to me. Not just here and there, but all the time. Glenn Roeder's words were ringing true. If you're successful up here, then you can be a hero. I was loving every minute of it and it was another learning curve for me. I was now being watched closely off the pitch as well as on it, but I was enjoying myself nonetheless.

I was feeling like I would score in every game I played. The bad times were surely behind me but just as I was getting into my stride, I was stopped in my tracks with Sunderland injury hell, part one.

Our next game was probably our stiffest challenge yet. A trip to St Andrews to face Birmingham City. I always find this fixture quite intimidating because they have a hostile following and their players are big, strong and never let you relax on the ball.

But we couldn't have gone into the game at a better time. So, typically, I go on to have one of my poorer games. I wasn't holding the ball up well and kept giving it away, which is a cardinal sin for a striker as far as the gaffer's concerned. He's very keen on his front men holding onto the ball, to bring others into the play, but it just wasn't happening for me. To make matters worse I should have scored with a header from a pin-point Mickey Gray cross but it just wasn't my day.

In the second-half, things were getting no better on a personal level then, in the 53rd minute I went up for a header and as I tried to lift off again, I felt something go in my leg. I spent the rest of the game sitting in the dug out but I was in pain. We went on to carve out a well earned victory, thanks to Mickey's low drive and we also ended Birmingham's 17-game unbeaten run in the process.

I went into the Washington Hospital that night, waking up every couple of hours to put ice on the injury. I had damaged my abductor muscle and was told it would take a month to heal, but it was while I was being assessed by the doctors that something far more serious was discovered.

While they were searching for my initial injury, they noticed that I had large lymph nodes growing in the glands in my groin. It was serious enough for the doctors to refer me to a specialist in Darlington. I was operated on to clear up the problem and although they didn't tell me at the time, it was thought that the nodes were cancerous. Thankfully this did not prove to be the case, but it put back my recovery time for another couple of weeks. I was in pain, and even more frustrating was the fact that I would be out of action for five games when, initially, I thought I'd only be out of action for no more than a fortnight.

The team kept up the winning momentum in my absence, with a 4–2 aggregate win against Bury in the Coca-Cola Cup. We also drew 1–1 in the league against Wolves, a game we should have won convincingly.

Young Michael Bridges came in for me and did a brilliant job, though. In training I soon discovered that he had more skill in his feet than the rest of us put together. Although he only scored once in my absence, he showed his class and if keeps his feet on the ground and his head right, I honestly think he can go on to become an England international, even if it now happens for him in the colours of Leeds United.

The only consolation for me was that I'd shown the management and the players what I could do. I was our top scorer and although I'd have to work hard for it, I was expecting to return to the side once I was fit. And the vibes I was getting off the management were good. In my three seasons at Sunderland, I've been injured for a total of five months and have never played a reserve game. That's the kind of faith that the management have in my ability and the best way to repay them is with goals.

It was also while I was out of the side that I found the benchmark we would have to reach if were to gain promotion at the end of the season. Our north-east neighbours Middlesbrough were the next visitors to the Stadium of Light and they brought plenty of fans to make the atmosphere inside the ground electric.

They went on to inflict our first defeat in seven games and they handed out a lesson in finishing that afternoon. Their Brazilian midfielder Emerson was running the show and I remember him scoring a great goal from fully 25 yards. We lost the game 2–1, with Kevin Ball grabbing a consolation in injury time. The fans were obviously disappointed, losing to their rivals, but we took a lot of positive things from the game. We now knew what we had to do to be up there with the best.

We were also beaten at Middlesbrough in the next round of the Coca-Cola Cup but due to a virus, we fielded a young side at the Riverside, so we didn't read too much into the game. But at this point, my mind was on other things. I was looking towards making my comeback at Reading.

The days were passing too quickly for me. It was now early October and although I was back in full training, I was still feeling a little jaded afterwards and wasn't sure if I was ready to return. Peter wanted to pitch me straight in for the game at Elm Park, but I told him that I wasn't 100 per cent and we agreed that I should start from the bench.

And I'm glad that I did because we chose 4 October 1997 to put in our worst performance during my time at the club. This was even more shocking than the game at Vale Park.

When I came on to the pitch to replace John Mullins with 15 minutes to go, we were already 4–0 down against a side which would go on to suffer relegation at the end of the season. Reading wanted the game more and were obviously lifted by probably their biggest crowd of the season. The scoreline didn't flatter Reading in the slightest. We were dreadful, but at least I had managed to put myself about a bit.

Back in the dressing room, the gaffer was letting fly with a barrage of four-letter words and rightly so. Thankfully, I wasn't on the receiving end, having only played for the last quarter of an hour. Quite the opposite happened, in fact.

The boss singled me out from the rest and, in front of everyone said, 'Look at this lad. He's been out injured for six weeks but managed to do more in the 15 minutes he was on the pitch than you lot did all game'. To be honest, it was a bit embarrassing. I didn't want to look like the teacher's pet, not while everyone was getting a right roasting, but it did make me feel good and I just wanted to show what I could do from the start next time.

Once everything had calmed down, we were getting whispers that our own fans were waiting to give us a roasting of their own. There were so many of them outside that we had to request a police escort onto the coach and, as anyone who can remember what Elm Park was like, there is no hiding place to quickly sneak onto the bus from a back exit.

I knew it would be bad, but I was completely shocked at just how fired up our fans were. It was then that I truly realised what their football club means to them. We were getting verbally abused, the air was thick blue! All I could hear was, 'You're shit, you're shit and you've been shit all season!' No-one was spared from the barrage of abuse, not even our kit man and former player John Cook. He thought he would just waltz onto the coach unrecognised but then someone yelled 'And you, you were shit when you played for us as well!' Although no-one dared laugh at the time, it was a funny moment to come out of a serious situation and we never let him forget it on the way home.

The vitriol continued as we pulled away from the ground, with some fans going as far as taking their Sunderland shirts off and throwing them at the coach. It was the scariest situation I'd found myself in at a football match. I honestly thought that a fan was going to land a punch on one of us and I was still shaking as we got back on the M4 for the long journey home.

As far as promotion was concerned, we were well off the pace. A year earlier Sunderland were contesting the likes of Man United and Arsenal. Now we were getting cleaned off the park by Reading. Something had to be done and fast.

And it was at that point that the new, improved Sunderland emerged. During training that week, frustration was boiling up in the players and instead of taking the defeats out on our opponents, the players were taking the defeats out on each other.

Steve Agnew and Richard Ord almost came to blows one day when they squared up to each other and had each other round the neck. Steve went berserk and I really thought he was going to hit Dicky, but we all managed to calm him down.

But something had to be done and the gaffer proceeded to drop a few of these more experienced heads. Richard went, likewise Andy Melville and Martin Scott, and in their place came Jody Craddock and Darren Williams as our centre-back pairing, Mickey Gray was put at left-back while Allan Johnston was brought in to fill the left midfield berth.

I'm not saying the players dropped wouldn't have responded to the Reading result, but the replacements gave a new look to the side. Everything was fresh again.

The players who came in knew that they had a job to do and would have to be at the top of their game if they were to remain in the side. Our next game was at home to Huddersfield and you could sense the new impetus in the side. We were alive again. The gaffer had pulled a masterstroke and the team never looked back. We would not lose for 17 matches and although it's easy to talk in hindsight, if we'd played with that team from the start of the campaign, I'm sure we would have walked the division. That bad, early run cost us dear.

Although it was a successful time for the side, on a personal level I was to endure my most barren run for the club. We comfortably beat Huddersfield 3–1, the highlight being Martin Smith's effort from 30 yards out, but in our next game, again at the Stadium of Light, I missed a penalty in a 0–0 draw against Swindon. It was at this point that I thought I would be rested. The team was winning without my goals and the goals were coming from all over the park. For instance, Lee Clark scored both the goals in a 2–1 win at Stoke, and netted in injury time the following week at Stockport, to salvage a 1–1 draw.

But as every striker and every manager knows, you are not going to score every week and I'm just pleased that Peter kept faith in me.

Thankfully the goal drought ended on 8 November at home to league leaders Nottingham Forest. We were still floating around in 10th place at this time and we had to get a result in an attempt to close the gap on them.

It took only two minutes for me to make my mark, when I rose at the far post to head home Martin Smith's deep cross. I would go on to score quite a few goals that season with my head, which surprises many people as I'm only 5ft 7in tall. But heading the ball is not just about height, it's about timing too. And I've never had a problem with that, even at an early age. I think my time as a defender at Southampton helped me too. As a right-back it was my duty to defend the back post and that gave me plenty of heading practice. It was all coming together now and heading remains a strong part of my game.

I rose above Forest's left-back Alan Rogers on this occasion and, as on my home debut, I celebrated my goal Klinsmann-style. We more than matched Forest that day but the game petered out to a 1–1 draw. Still, we knew that if we could put together a run of wins, we had the ability and the determination to join them at the top.

I had my taste for goals back and following our 4–1 win at Portsmouth, scored in the 1–1 draw at Bury and in our 3–0 romp at home to Tranmere.

But then football went on the back burner for a while. On 2 December, our first child, Millie, was born. Thankfully we hadn't set out for our trip to Queens Park Rangers at this point and I was able to witness the birth. I had never seen anything more fascinating in all my life. Julie was only in labour for four hours and everything went smoothly.

I felt like the proudest person on earth and although my life wouldn't change dramatically, I now had a major responsibility on my hands. Those early days were quite nerve-wracking as we had no family around us, but Julie was brilliant and those sleepless nights didn't really affect me on the pitch. I was on such a high.

I wet the baby's head that Wednesday night in Durham and had more than the odd pint of Guinness and glass of champagne with Andy Melville, with whom I had grown to become good friends.

I turned up late for training the next day. I think I was still drunk. And just as the gaffer walked towards me, probably ready to fine me and give me a good roasting, I said, 'Gaffer, I'm a Dad'. He was elated for me and so were the rest of the lads. I just couldn't wait for the QPR game where we were all set for a 'Bebeto-style' celebration if we scored.

We did manage to score at Rangers. Niall Quinn cut inside their full-back Steve Morrow to drill the ball home with five minutes to go and we won 1–0. We must have had around 6,000 fans at Loftus Road that day and as the ground is so cramped, they all came running on the pitch. We were mobbed and we couldn't even celebrate normally, let alone Bebeto-style. That was a shame, but at least we'd got another three points. It was three wins from four now and the world seemed wonderful, for me and for the team.

I felt at ease with myself, there was no more worry over the birth. I was also at ease with my team-mates. Everyone was now familiar with their roles and we all felt more relaxed when we stepped out on to the pitch. It was almost like we knew we were going to win every game we played. The niggling doubts that we had in the back of our heads earlier in the season were now a distant memory.

It was no coincidence, then, that I would now score in seven consecutive games, the first Sunderland player to do so since Bobby Gurney in 1930. But, in all honesty, it was harder for me not to score. The crosses which were raining in from Nicky Summerbee and Allan Johnston were first class and I was picking up so many scraps.

Up until Christmas 1997, we won three consecutive games against West Brom, Crewe and Bradford. The only blot on the list was a 1–1 draw at Oxford where I stuck out a leg from a Summerbee shot and Lionel Perez saved us from defeat with a great, late save.

We were winning and it was Christmas. A time for eating, drinking, relaxing and partying. Not any more.

Believe it or not, this was the first Christmas I'd had to play through, having been injured at Watford for the other two seasons, and it did seem a bit strange when you saw everyone out and enjoying themselves while we prepared for three games in eight days. But if it meant that we would be promoted at the end of the season, then it would be a small price to pay.

We did manage to celebrate at the club with a disco for the players and wives, but it was nothing too heavy because we knew such a lot was at stake. If we could get ourselves into the Premiership, then they'd be plenty of time to celebrate during the summer.

Our final game of the festive period was a trip to Rotherham in the third round of the FA Cup, a game in which I was not feeling confident for some reason. There are always two or three shocks in the third round and on a sticky pitch, away from home, I thought an upset might be on the cards.

I needn't have worried. It was one of those days where everything I touched seemed to end up in the back of the net. Bang. Goal number one was a penalty. Then two, three, four. Four goals for the first time in my professional career and we had romped to a 5–1 win. Just who is this Kevin Phillips? Now the national press boys were on my case and I was getting quite a lot of publicity. Well, it's not every day you score four goals in a cup tie.

I equalled Gurney's record on 17 January, at struggling Man City. And what a game to do it in. Maine Road was, as usual, packed out and the atmosphere was fabulous. Like St Andrew's, the City support can give you a rough ride, but having scored another two goals in the final ten minutes of our previous game – a 4–2 win at home to Sheffield United – I was feeling good.

And it's a good job I was in tip-top shape because the local press had been building the game up all week. Will Super Kev break the record? Will he write his name into the Sunderland record books? The pressure was hotting up but, to be honest, I didn't even know until the start of the week that I was on the verge of equalling a record. I certainly had no idea who Bobby Gurney was.

The game was also special as Peter Reid was back at the club which sacked him. He was fired up, I was fired up and another three points would put us firmly back in the play-off frame. The game itself was tight, with very few chances, but somehow I managed to put away another header when I timed my leap to perfection to meet Nicky's cross. When the City defender mistimed his jump and the ball connected with my head, I knew it was going in straight away.

Get in there! I'd done it, and the feeling was brilliant. I just ran away celebrating, right in front of the City fans, not a wise thing to do at the best of times, certainly not when I knew I had won us the game. But I didn't care, I was back up on Cloud Nine again.

When the game had finished, a representative from Nationwide approached me and wanted to present me with a bottle of champagne in front of our travelling supporters behind one of the goals. After winding the home fans up so much, I was not sure whether to do it, in case one of them came onto the pitch to attack me, but I cautiously agreed.

And I'm pleased I did it because all our fans stayed behind and one end of Maine Road was chanting 'Super Kev' loud and proud. It was the most satisfying moment of my six months on Wearside and a photograph of the occasion now hangs high and proud in my new home today.

When I came off the pitch, the press were swarming around me asking me how I felt, but I had to answer them honestly and said that it was just another goal. I had won Sunderland another three points and that was all that really mattered.

Records and personal achievements are for when you've packed up playing. Of course it's an honour to score in seven consecutive games, but it's something I'll appreciate more when I'm going through my scrapbooks with my children and grandchildren.

I wonder what Chris Nicholl was thinking now. But

who knows? If I'd been given that contract at Southampton, maybe I wouldn't have been so determined to succeed as I now was. Maybe it was a blessing in disguise because I was now living in dreamworld. Fame, fortune and goals all rolled into one.

Even the television companies wanted a piece of the action. I was invited down to appear on Sky's Saturday morning programme 'Soccer AM' and as it was live, I was a bit nervous to start with but it was quite a laugh, really. The problems started when I got back home because the lads slaughtered me for wearing a Diadora tracksuit. Julie said I looked really pale and the gaffer thought I had been on the bottle. And they're supposed to be on my side! From now on, I have to wear designer clothes and get the make-up artists to work on my face, and that's before I even start to talk football.

Going out in town was also proving to be more difficult. Of course, it's nice to speak to the fans and I'm always happy to sign autographs, but there are times when you want to be alone and just enjoy a quiet meal with family or friends.

Our home, too, backed on to quite a large estate in Brancepeth and word soon got around that Kevin Phillips lived in the area. Having people knock on the door was not really that much of a problem to me, but with a new-born baby in the house trying to sleep, it was causing us some concern. With the baby also keeping us awake during the night, it was getting quite tough for us new parents, but Julie was brilliant and when I had a game coming up, she would tend to Millie's every need. I can't thank her enough for that but we knew we had to move again quite soon, just to get some privacy. Such is the price of fame!

I also had to be more careful when going out up the road in Newcastle. Many more people knew who I was and who I played for and I remember going into the cubicle of a toilet in one of the Newcastle bars when I heard three lads behind me say, 'That's Kevin Phillips, he plays for Sunderland'. I thought that was it, someone was about to turn my lights out for the night. But as I turned around they said, 'It's okay, if you get into any trouble, we'll look out for you'. They were Sunderland fans.

I stopped sweating but I know where I can and cannot go out in Newcastle now. I've been to the Quayside a few times with the rest of the lads and the atmosphere's good down there, but I know that if I ventured further into town, into the Bigg Market, I doubt whether I would come out alive! That's the extreme passion and rivalry which exists between Sunderland and Newcastle fans. They wouldn't have it any other way. And we were edging ever closer towards playing Newcastle the following season in the Premiership.

Unfortunately, we didn't have an FA Cup run to look forward to anymore. Our first defeat in almost three months came at Tranmere in the fourth round. The record shows that we've never won at Prenton Park and this was our sixth successive defeat there. I missed a sitter which could have put us through, and it would have set us up with a mouth-watering fifth round tie at St James' Park. Oh well, at least we had the league to concentrate on now.

But if we'd suffered the curse of Tranmere Rovers, we also had the curse of Norwich City to contend with now. Four days after our cup exit we travelled the long journey to Carrow Road and were beaten 2–1, despite a 25-yard strike from Lee Clark. Apart from Middlesbrough, they were the only team to do the double on us, and it was a quiet, maybe even a little concerned, group of players who trekked back home.

Those long coach journeys can become really monotonous and I think we travelled by coach to almost every game that season, even the trip down to Portsmouth, which is by far the longest trip of all. Mind you, I can't complain about the quality of our coach company – Moor Dale – which, in fact we share with Newcastle.

Seats and tables at the front. Microwave, fridge and couch at the back, it's all quite impressive. To pass the time, I usually watch videos down the front with Allan Johnston, while at the back, the card school is in full operation. It didn't take long for me to work out that Niall Quinn, Andy Melville, Michael Bridges, Paul Butler and Bobby Saxton were the card kings. Mickey Gray was supposed to be the entertainment's manager, to sort out the music and the videos for the rest of us, but I think that lasted five minutes!

Coming back from Norfolk, the talk was of promotion. Okay, we'd had a couple of wobbles but as the gaffer said, 'You are playing good, attacking football and if we continue in the same vein, we won't be far off a promotion place'. I agreed entirely and I truly believe that the football we were playing during this period was better than anything we achieved during our championship season. We were hitting teams by three, four, even five goals and conceding very little. If only we could keep it going for the remainder of the season.

We responded brilliantly with a 4–2 home win against Port Vale which consolidated our fourth place position. I managed to score again but was overshadowed by Quinny who scored with a beautiful lob from 20 yards out.

We followed up with a vital smash-and-grab win at Wolves, with Kevin Ball grabbing the only goal of the game. It was then that we really thought we could go all the way and grab an automatic promotion slot.

Each season I set myself a target of 20 goals and managed to reach that target the following week as we exacted revenge on Reading. But now it was crunch time, Middlesbrough were waiting for us at the Riverside. If we could win, we were really in the driving seat.

This was, without doubt, our biggest game of the season. I was nervous before the game and I could sense that a few of the less experienced lads were feeling the same. That's when you need the likes of Quinny and the skipper Kevin Ball to give you a few words of encouragement and it was all positive stuff. 'Win this one and we've got the upper hand,' said Bally. 'Beat them in their own backyard and we could be on our way.'

What happened was nothing short of a catastrophe. We were second best to everything and Boro cruised into a 3–0 lead. They were by far the better side and we hardly created a thing. I had a poor game and was brought off. The whole match left a bitter taste in my mouth but I can't play well and score in every game.

We did grab a late consolation through Lee Clark but now it was Boro who had the upper hand. But the gaffer was not too hard on us after the game. I think even he realised that Middlesbrough were *the* outstanding team of the season. They were strong in every department, had a team of internationals and had twice beaten us convincingly in the league. In my opinion, they deserved to go up as champions and we still had some way to go to be on a par with them.

CHAPTER FOUR

The Road To Wembley

Allan Johnston had grown to become a big friend of mine during my time in the north-east. For a Scotsman, he's a quiet, laid-back kind of guy, which is unusual, and we seemed to hit it off from the start. So much so that we began rooming together on away trips and even sat together on the team coach to away games.

But one day I was far too generous for my own good. Having licked our wounds against Middlesbrough, the final, big push for promotion took us, first, to the McAlpine Stadium in Huddersfield. We were playing well and Johnno was on course for his hat-trick, having scored twice already. We were then awarded a penalty before half-time and instead of banging the ball home myself, I handed the ball over to my big mate so that he could grab his glory. Little did I know that come the end of the season, that decision would cost me the chance of finishing as Division One's outright leading scorer with 30 league goals. Instead, I had to share that honour with

Nottingham Forest's Pierre Van Hooijdonk, so if you're reading this Johnno, remember you owe me one!

To add insult to injury, the boss brought me off that day. I was beginning to feel a little concerned. This was the most important stage of the season for me, but I had gone two games without a goal and wasn't playing well. Did I have the stomach for the fight? Was I bottling the big games, such as Middlesbrough? I thought I had what it takes, but what about the management and the fans?

I spoke to the boss about it and he assured me that I had done him proud and had proved to be one of his bests buys. He just said, 'Keep working hard and the goals will come'. It was the reassurance I needed but I helped myself by spending a little longer after training, just working on my game by firing a few balls at our young keepers. As I've said, training at Sunderland is not that strenuous. With the way we play, the emphasis is more on ball work, so for much of the week we play five-a-sides and work on sprints. Preparing for our opponents comes later in the week as the big game approaches and, usually, training doesn't last for much more than an hour-and-a-half. That's why I spend some time on my own, just sharpening up in front of goal. It's a tip I'd give any aspiring striker, because nothing gives you more confidence than slamming a few balls into the back of the net. You also get to see and hear things from the goalkeeper's perspective. Practice makes perfect, after all.

And I was back on the goal trail the very next game, netting our equaliser with an overhead kick in the 50th minute against Ipswich. Unfortunately, we could only draw the game 2–2 but the disappointment was eased by the fact that I was back and had scored against one of the best teams in the division. Bottling the big stage? Not a chance.

The top two, Nottingham Forest and Middlesbrough were due to meet live on TV the following day, and Sky had invited me to be a guest in their Isleworth studio for the game. So there was no time for any post-match drinks to celebrate my return to form, I had to dash to Durham to catch the 6.15 pm train to Stevenage, stay overnight at my Mum's and then onto the studio the following morning.

Forget first class. I didn't have time. I just grabbed a ticket and found a seat. Little did I know that the train would be packed with Ipswich fans and exiled Mackems, returning to London. So, to avoid any embarrassing situations, I just tried to keep my head down and sat in my seat. Trouble is, that's never easy when the journey takes almost three hours and you are starving and thirsty, having just played 90 minutes of professional football.

So after about an hour, I just had to get something to eat and headed for the buffet bar, in the next carriage. But as I was waiting in the queue, I could sense that people were staring at me. I daren't look round but I could sense the burning sensation of their eyes in the back of my head. Then, there was the inevitable tap on the shoulder and the words, 'You're Kevin Phillips, aren't you?' I felt like saying 'No' but I didn't have the heart, so just smiled, said 'yes' very quietly and returned to my seat to get stuck into my sandwich.

Ten minutes later, pandemonium breaks out and I am surrounded by between 15 and 20 members of the Sunderland Supporters' Club, London branch. They wouldn't leave me alone for the rest of the journey, buying me food and, more importantly, a few beers. After the initial embarrassment, we turned out to have quite a laugh and there were handshakes all round as the train stopped at Stevenage.

I jumped off at the top of the platform, some way up from the station's exit and, little did I know, my new mates had got off too, a couple of carriages down. They were waiting for me by the station's steps and, just as I looked up, they started chanting 'Super Kev' at the top of their voices as I walked towards them.

My Mum had come to pick me up and she must have known that I was on my way, but it was a brilliant moment that I'll never forget and it again showed just how special our fans are.

Forest went on to comfortably beat Middlesbrough, leaving the door open nicely for us to take advantage. And for the record, I might have had a few ales the night before but my second appearance on Sky was far better than the first. No more tracksuits, no more pasty faces, just my lucky blue velvet suit and a smile. The lads were far happier with me this time!

Learning to deal with the media is a big part of football today. The press, TV and radio are in your face every day at Sunderland because we are such a big club. But I've never had a problem with them and, to be honest, I quite enjoy expressing my opinions and enjoy the TV work I get from time to time.

With regards to the press, I think I share the same opinions as Kevin Keegan. I believe that if you are fair, honest and open with them, they will respond and treat you in the same way. I appreciate that they have a job to do, but I also appreciate not every player shares that view and my feelings could well change if things start to go wrong. In any case, the football media is going to get bigger and bigger as the game continues to grow in this country and it would be a good idea if the young pros are given a bit more help in this area. Media training would be a good idea, because it's hard enough trying to make your name in the game when you're young, without all the added pressure the media can bring.

The Sky cameras were certainly following us closely at this stage of the season. The following week, we were back in people's living rooms again. Nottingham Forest at the City Ground. A massive game. We simply had to win to keep the pressure on, but Dave Bassett's men were in the form of their lives and playing at home. In the dressing room, the lads were well up for it and after we saw the incredible support that had come to the City Ground, there was only going to be one winner.

We chose Forest to put in our best performance of the season and never looked in trouble once Alex Rae had opened the scoring on the half hour. Johnno then scored one of the goals of the season with a lovely chip from the edge of the box in the second half and I scored from close range in the final ten minutes. But you couldn't single anyone out for praise that day, the whole side was superb and I had a feeling that everything was coming together at the right time. We were going up.

I kept my scoring run going in the next game, too, as we easily disposed of Stockport 4–1 with Quinny grabbing a hat-trick. We had moved into an automatic promotion place for the first time all season. The matches were coming thick and fast and three days later Birmingham were the visitors to the Stadium of Light.

We just couldn't keep up the relentless pace and got ourselves out of jail when Johnno converted Quinny's knockdown in the 90th minute to salvage a point. We had drawn 1–1 and you could sense that the players were starting to tire a little bit. We needed a break, not just to get away from the football but to get away from the pressures that the press and the fans bring, too.

So it was off to sunny Bournemouth for relaxation, a bit of light training and plenty of golf. I was in my element, playing golf and forgetting about football for a while. Nearly all the lads at the club play the game and if I could turn back the clock, I would have preferred to have been a golfer than a footballer.

When I was at Watford, I got down to a four handicap at one point but since Millie's been born, I tend to spend a lot of my spare time with her rather than on the golf course. But I still enjoy the odd round and usually have close battles with Niall Quinn, who is a good golfer.

I'm often asked what I'll do when I pack up playing football and I'd love to get on the Challenge Tour at some point. I've heard that Julian Dicks is trying to turn professional and it would be great to see him succeed. Who knows, I might even try to follow in his path. I'll certainly have the time on my hands.

But I was a bit bemused as to why we chose

Bournemouth for our break. Although it's a lovely place, it couldn't be much further from Sunderland and it took nearly a day for us to get there by coach.

It did, however, turn out to be the best break I've had in my time at Sunderland, if only to see Quinny's drinking antics at close hand. We had a tough and very important game at Charlton on the Sunday and the gaffer restricted us to just one night's drinking. It was Wednesday night and we all split up to go our own ways. I didn't fancy just drinking the night away, so I went to play a bit of snooker with a couple of the lads in a local club. A couple of hours later, we came out and decided to head back to the hotel to see if any of the other lads were about. The place was dead but rumours were quickly circulating that it was all happening in O'Neill's, the Irish bar in town. So we quickly rushed down, and there, propping up the bar, was the main man, Quinny.

There was a general rule in the pub that if you could drink 14 pints of Guinness, you had your name up in lights at the bar. Unbelievably, Quinny had downed 16 pints and although he had gone out in a white jumper, it was now black. He had a big Guinness hat on his head and was singing Irish songs. It was an unbelievable sight and we all sat back, amazed that he was still standing.

Our kit-man John Cook and masseur Michael Holland helped carry him home and with an important training session planned for the morning, we weren't holding out much hope for poor Niall.

But, amazingly, Quinny was up and raring to go. With Charlton fast emerging on the horizon, the gaffer put us through a tough workout with plenty of running and somehow. Niall was putting the work in as if he'd been tucked up in bed at 9.00 pm the previous night. It was an amazing sight and I've never seen anything quite like it before. Respect, Quinny!

Like us, Charlton were putting a run together. We had drawn 0–0 earlier in the season but they were looking for a play-off place now, while we were looking for automatic promotion. It was not going to be a game without incident.

We got off to a great start with another textbook header from yours truly, but the game was turned on its head after a disgraceful decision by the referee, who sent off Alex Rae for merely running into his opponent.

The sacrificial lamb that afternoon turned out to be me and I was stuck in midfield as we tried to defend our lead. Lamb? I was more like a headless chicken running about, I didn't know what was going on. It was like having that trial at Barnet all over again.

Mark Bright grabbed their equaliser and the game was drawn. Poor Alex received a bollocking off the boss for his performance, but I don't think he had seen the harshness of the sending off at this point. Frustration was the best word to describe the dressing room afterwards.

We almost threw away the following game, too, against Portsmouth. Another headed goal had come my way, but Darren Williams and Lionel Perez were involved in a crazy mix up at the back which looked like putting us further behind Middlesbrough and Forest in what was now clearly a three-horse race to the top.

But cometh the man, cometh the hour. It was Johnno to the rescue with a late curler into the top corner. He might miss ten similar attempts throughout any given month, but he usually puts one away. A cross, maybe. A goal, definitely. Another three points, no question.

Now I'm not saying that we're a team of alcoholics but like many football clubs, the players like to socialise and at Sunderland, we do it all together. It makes for a tremendous team spirit, which is clearly evident when we take to the pitch. We then beat Bury 2–1, and as our next game was at Tranmere on Merseyside on a Friday night – the day before the Grand National – a trip to Aintree was a formality.

But the football had to come first and we had to bury that Prenton Park hoodoo. We got off to a great start when I tucked home Quinny's through ball after five minutes and just six minutes later the game was over as a spectacle when Nicky Summerbee blasted home my cross. From then on, it wasn't pretty stuff as it was cold and the pitch was sticky, but we held out for the 2–0 win and I was in the mood to celebrate.

I was feeling lucky, and a nice little earner on the horses would make my weekend. So the tickets were bought and we arrived at the racecourse at around midday. Two hours, yes two hours later we finally bowled through the turnstiles – I now know how our fans must feel when they queue for tickets at the Stadium of Light. But this was a hot day, and naturally we were in need of some liquid refreshment. An Irish Bar immediately hit us in the face but as we got nearer, the queue for beers was 40-deep. This was fast turning into a nightmare and although a large contingent of the players and their mates stayed, a few of us cut our losses and walked out without putting on a bet or even bothering to stay and watch the big race itself.

The fact that a huge pub down the road had caught our eye on the way in, might have had something to do with our decision. It had a big screen from which to watch the race and we ended up drinking champagne, wine and whatever else came our way. The lads who stayed for the race came out empty handed, and so did we, but you could tell which ones had had the better afternoon!

Sunday was spent nursing hangovers but at least we didn't have a midweek game to worry about, just Queens Park Rangers on the Friday night, live on Sky.

I say just QPR, but as far as the lads were concerned this was the biggest game of the season for us. From all the matches I have played in – bar the game at Wembley – I've never known a more intense build up to a game than this one. All we did that week was talk about the game because we knew that if we could win, we were confident that we could go on and get automatic promotion.

I wouldn't say we were anxious because of the importance but we weren't our normal selves. The game was played on a Friday night, which messed up our normal routine and although we had gone 2–0 up through two well taken Niall Quinn goals and were cruising to victory, the second half went badly wrong. The swirling wind and rain made conditions very difficult and we decided to commit promotional suicide.

Rangers striker Mike Sheron is a proven goalscorer and looked lively all game. He went on to score two goals in the last 15 minutes, the first when he pounced on a poor Chris Makin back pass and the second, just seven minutes from time when he shot low under Perez. The game was drawn, but it might as well have been lost. An eerie silence cast itself over our stadium and the mood in the dressing was one of huge disappointment and disbelief. Bins were being kicked and the air was blue. But there was nothing we could do now, it was over.

'Just forget it,' said the gaffer. 'We've blown it because of stupid individual mistakes. That's what's cost us, nothing else.' We couldn't afford anymore mistakes but that game really put the mockers on us, and we didn't really recover our true form again that season.

But if we'd committed suicide in that game, then our trip to the Hawthorns saw the nails inserted into the coffin. To be blunt, our first-half performance was awful and we were being pulled all over the place.

We were 2–0 down within 11 minutes and rightly so. Lee Hughes and Kevin Kilbane were causing us problems and both hit the target. We didn't want another roasting off the gaffer at half-time, so had to pull something out of the bag and quick to turn things around.

Which is exactly what happened. Out came our true colours and we staged an incredible fight back. First it was hot-shot Quinny, who converted another of Johnno's crosses and then I levelled things up on the half hour when two of their defenders decided to collide into each other, leaving me with the simplest of finishes. We'd even had Mickey Gray sent off at this point but just didn't want the half to end.

In the dressing room the gaffer kept reminding us of how hard we'd worked with ten men against Charlton. Let's just hope that we could hold out this time.

The omens were looking good when Quinny scored again, lobbing the ball home from the edge of the box soon after the re-start. But with ten men, I was again sacrificed and put back into midfield as we tried to consolidate and hold on to our lead. But it was not to be. Hughes equalised in the dying moments of the game and the dressing room was a scene of utter devastation. Again. Finishing third was even under threat now.

That game still leaves a bitter taste in my mouth. When I look back over the season, I can't help but wonder how we would have got on that day if I'd been left to play up front with Quinny. Attacking is the strongest part of our game and if we'd just gone for more goals instead of sitting back, trying to hold out, we may well have collected all three points. I can understand the reasons why the management put me into midfield again, but I would have felt happier pushing forward, rather than trying to defend. It would be my only criticism of our tactics during the entire two seasons, which says so much for the management skills of Peter Reid and Bobby Saxton.

Sendings off were also costing us dear. This time it was Mickey. And instead of receiving a club fine at Sunderland, you have to take the team our for a nice meal and pick up the tab at the end of the evening.

Mickey's 'punishment' was to take us all out to an Italian restaurant on the seafront. Naturally, the gaffer was there because it was free and we were all making the most of Mickey's generosity. Naturally, we were buying the £15 bottles of wine and you could see that our 'host' was wincing with every bottle drunk. It was really getting to him, so to wind him up even further, we were filling up the empties with water while he wasn't looking. Then, after we'd grabbed his attention, we started pouring the 'wine' out of the window. He went absolutely mad and I don't think we told him the true story until the next day.

Again, that afternoon typified the spirit we have at the club and it's great that we have a manager who is such a big part of the camaraderie. But it proved to be an expensive outing for our flying left-back and needless to say, nobody got themselves sent off again all season!

Back on the football pitch, everything I seemed to touch ended up in the back of the net. I had earned my first international call-up, for the England B team against Russia, and I felt on top of the world. It was also a time for more record breaking. I went into our game with Stoke knowing that if I scored I would be the first player to reach 30 goals in a season since the legend of Brian Clough some 36 years earlier. I was feeling so confident of reaching that target that I wore a T-shirt with '30' written on it, underneath my Sunderland shirt. I hit a post just before half-time and although Darren Williams had already made it 1–0, I thought that it was just going to be one of those days.

But after the re-start, history was in the making. A quick pass from Johnno and I was in on goal and managed to slip the ball past the on-rushing Neville Southall. To beat a man of his stature was a highlight for me, but to score the big three-zero was something else. Up went the shirt and the fans went wild. I don't think I came back down to earth for a good five minutes as the players mobbed me.

I managed to grab a second in the final minute, taking advantage of a Lee Clark blocked shot and I just wish I'd had another shirt made up with '31' on it.

The press attention after the game was unbelievable. It was another one of those evenings when I didn't get away from the stadium until about 8.00 pm. To get 30 goals was a massive achievement, considering this was my first season at the club and I'd been out injured for a while, too. I ended the season with a total of 35 goals and it's a club post-war record which will, I hope, stand for a long time. I thought I might have received a message or a fax from Cloughie but nothing came through. But I hope that he's proud and impressed with the achievement.

The Sky jinx hit us again on the Tuesday night when we crashed 2–0 at Ipswich. The first-half was tight and I had few chances to make an impression. They took the lead just after the re-start with a Matt Holland diving header and should have made it two when David Johnson took a dive in the box and Alex Mathie missed the resulting penalty. But he made amends on the hour with a volley and that finished us off.

It was now two wins from five – not promotion form in anyone's book. Ipswich were now looking strong for the play-offs and took the initiative that evening while we didn't seem to be performing on the big stage. It was a concern for us all and the gaffer was not happy. He wanted to know where our bottle had gone. 'If we can't handle this kind of atmosphere, how would you do against the big boys?' I remember him saying. A good question. Were we ready? Probably not. We were a young side still learning our trade. We were far from the finished article at this stage.

Nottingham Forest had already been crowned champions, so it had become a straight battle between ourselves and Middlesbrough for the second automatic play-off spot. But we had blown it at the final hurdle. A win at Portman Road could have sent us on our way, but now we had to win at Swindon on the final day of the season and hope that Oxford would get a result at the Riverside.

Our destiny was now out of our hands. It was a horrible situation to find ourselves in, having got into contention right up until the final week but we had to just concentrate on our own game down at the County Ground.

Andy Melville knew a few of the Oxford lads and had given them a call during the week and they said they'd be trying their best to win, but we knew before we even stepped out onto the pitch that we would have to settle for the play-offs.

Like so many of our away games at the smaller grounds, our fans came in their hordes and I think they filled almost three of the four stands. We had to put in a good final performance for them as much as anyone and we duly obliged. I managed to score our two goals before half-time and the first was, without doubt, the best of my 35 that season.

The game was 20 minutes old and I managed to bring

the ball down on my chest before hitting a volley on the turn from the edge of the box which flew past their keeper Frazer Digby. The second goal came as the half-time whistle blew, a blast from close range.

Could those goals send us up? Highly unlikely, but could Oxford really pull off the impossible? Maybe they could. As we went in at the break, we found out that they were holding Middlesbrough 0–0.

The second-half was just 30 seconds old when the news filtered through that the inevitable had happened. The Swindon fans were singing loud and proud and you could see on the faces of our supporters that we would be consigned to the play-offs.

Middlesbrough romped to a 4–1 victory. We had won 2–1. But far from shedding tears, our fans showed their true colours by singing loud and proud themselves as the end of the game approached. When the final whistle blew, they stormed onto the pitch and we were made to feel like heroes. I was carried back to the dressing room on their shoulders and although it was a great feeling, it was quite scary having dozens of drunk men throwing themselves at you. I remember even getting caught in the face by one of them trying to get my shirt. It took a good ten or so minutes to get back in the dressing room but there wasn't the despondency you might have expected. That had already let itself out at Portman Road. There were no tears to be shed, just a determination to beat Sheffield United in our play-off semi-final and then make it to Wembley for the big one.

But it was Forest and Middlesbrough who took their place in the top-flight. In all fairness, I thought Bryan

Robson's men would win the championship, simply for the fact that they played so well against us. Not only that, they had an abundance of star names like Andy Townsend, Paul Merson and, towards the end of the campaign, Paul Gascoigne. From the two sides, I knew they were the team with the infrastructure to do well in the Premiership and that's proved to be the case. We, too, knew we had the finances, the stadium and the squad to make a real go of life in the top-flight. That was chairman Bob Murray and Peter Reid's ambition from the moment we were relegated. But it was not going to be easy. Sheffield United over two legs and then a big game at Wembley. Everything was hanging in the balance. Our entire season hinged on the next two, hopefully, three games.

We had a week to prepare for United and I fancied our chances against them, having beaten them quite comfortably at the Stadium of Light at the turn of the year. The fact that we would have home advantage in the second leg also tipped the balance of the tie in our favour, but we knew we had to keep it tight in the first game at Bramall Lane.

The atmosphere there was electric; two big teams with great fans giving it their all in a bid to get back in the big time. We started the game comfortably and looked like we would get a result, a scoring draw at the very least. It was inevitable that we would score first and I had a part in the build-up, knocking the ball down for our skipper Kevin Ball to drill the ball home from the edge of the box.

In all fairness, it was my only contribution of the

game. I was having a bad time of it and was duly roasted at half-time, and told to sort myself out and stop giving the ball away. I just didn't know what was wrong with me. Maybe it was because Quinny was out injured and as I hadn't played that many games alongside Danny Dichio things weren't clicking. Maybe it was the occasion. But, no matter how hard I tried, I just couldn't get with the pace of the game and continued to struggle.

It wasn't just me. Our goal seemed to spark the opposition into life instead of motivating us and United hit us with two second-half goals. Their nippy Brazilian, Marcelo, ghosted in to score from a corner and the Greek lad Borbokis bent a free-kick around the wall to score from 25 yards. We had collapsed. It was just a case of not conceding anymore. Thankfully that proved to be the case but, again, we'd lost a crunch game.

The talk afterwards was that we needed to have gone up automatically as we didn't have the heart or the stomach for the big, one-off games. Self doubt was inevitably creeping in and I'm sure the gaffer was thinking the same, but this was the wrong time for condemnation. We had to stick together as a unit for the second leg. We had a point to prove to ourselves and to our critics.

Thankfully we only had three days to wait for the game at the Stadium of Light. I don't think I could have waited another week in anticipation.

It was to be the biggest game the new stadium would hold all season. It was like the Ajax game all over again with fans milling about outside a good two to three hours before the kick-off. I'm sure most people were expecting us to win, and many fans had already planned their day out at Wembley. But the Twin Towers had to be forgotten about as far as the players were concerned.

When we ran out at the start of the game, the atmosphere was the best I'd ever witnessed at a football match. I remember looking at Johnno and he just shook his head in disbelief. There was also a mist which had built up over the pitch to add to the occasion and everything was in place for a cracking game of football. We just had to make sure that we were the victors. This was our chance to show that when it comes to the crunch, we had what it takes to win. It was time to bury the 'big game' hoodoo.

This was to be my best game at the Stadium of Light that season – there was no way I was going to throw away my chance of playing in the Premiership without a fight.

We went 1–0 up after 20 minutes when Johnno's shot was deflected in by United defender Nicky Marker and that settled our nerves. The scores were 2–2 on aggregate and we were ahead on the away goals rule, but instead of just sitting back this time, we went for the kill. And it paid off. As the half came to a close, Nicky Summerbee had a shot which looked like it was going to hit the corner flag, so to save his embarrassment, I stuck out a leg and the ball flew in past their keeper Simon Tracey. Unbelievable, but let's not forget, they only needed a goal and the match would be all-square again. Wembley was still 45 minutes away for both sides.

My old Watford team-mate David Holdsworth just

had to ruin things for me, didn't he. With 15 minutes to go he gave me such a painful dead leg that I had to leave the pitch. I could hardly walk, let alone run. Cheers 'Reg'. But was this part of their game plan to unsettle us? Whatever, the substitution worked in their favour as we lost our shape a little bit.

As I sat in the back of the dugout, I just had a feeling they would equalise as they were pushing more and more men forward. Thankfully, Lionel Perez was on his game and in the very last minute pulled off one of the best saves I've ever seen, it was true Gordon Banks stuff. Graham Stuart hit a volley and although Lionel was wrong-footed, he managed to get down to his right post and palm the ball away. It fell into the path of one of their strikers and I'd already consigned myself to the agony of having to watch an extra 30 minutes. But then as the ball was heading goalbound, Lionel managed to push the ball out for a corner. Incredible.

When the final whistle went, the fans remained in their seats, limiting the risk of another punch in the face and it gave us the chance to thank them all for their tremendous support that season.

That was it, we were on our way to Wembley. I was to play at the famous old stadium for the first time in my career. Of course, it made up for the disappointment of missing out on automatic promotion, but I would have gladly sacrificed the chance of a Wembley trip for the guarantee that we would be playing the likes of Manchester United and Arsenal the following season.

I think that was the general mood in the dressing room afterwards, but what will be will be. We were going to Wembley and we were going to enjoy it. There was no champagne or singing as we got changed. Celebrations were low key and after the game I just went with Julie for an Indian meal in Durham with Danny Dichio and his girlfriend. If there was any celebrating to be done, we would have to wait at least another 90 minutes for it.

The Wembley game couldn't come quick enough for us. We had picked up momentum again and, but for the second half at Bramall Lane, were playing well. What disappointed me was the fact that we would now have to wait another two weeks before the final against Charlton, who had beaten Ipswich in their semi-final. Anything could happen in that time: injury, illness, loss of form. I just wanted to play the game. We owed Charlton for that defeat at The Valley. I was ready for them and there was absolutely no way I would find myself in midfield this time.

CHAPTER FIVE

Gray Day

In my opinion, the First Division play-off final at Wembley is a far bigger match than the stadium's showpiece game, the FA Cup final. There is far more at stake, with a place in the Premiership the prize. Players and managers want to test themselves against the game's elite, in Europe's most exciting league. Chairmen and directors know promotion will guarantee a cash windfall. And for the fans, nearly all are guaranteed a ticket for this game, making for an atmosphere rarely seen at the old stadium.

With so much at stake, you would expect a tight, even affair with the odd goal separating the finalists. But in most of the First Division play-off games I've seen, they've been absolute crackers. Swindon against Leicester sticks in the memory, the game where Glenn Hoddle ran the show for The Robins, while Reading versus Bolton was another match in which there was plenty of goal action. These two games were high-scoring affairs, and contenders for 'Game of the Nineties' but the match on 25 May 1998 proved to be the greatest of the last ten years, and possibly the finest ever witnessed at Wembley.

It was the turn of Sunderland and Charlton to end season 1997/98 with a bang. It was certainly the biggest game of my career and I'm sure it was the same for many of the other players on the pitch that day. As a young lad, I would watch the big Cup finals and England games on TV and really envy the players as they walked out of the Wembley tunnel and into the cauldron of noise.

I'd only ever been to the stadium for a guided tour when I was about ten but could vividly remember walking up the steps to lift some replica Cup as a tape of 100,000 screaming fans was played to an empty stadium. I also remember walking around the big dressing rooms, looking into the gigantic baths and running up the tunnel. It was a fairytale but now I would be living that dream. But it seemed to take forever to come.

With the enforced break between the semi-final and the final, the gaffer took us away for four days to Mottram Hall near Manchester to prepare .

Our timetable was split between playing golf, swimming, gym work and training, and drinking was certainly off the agenda this time. I would have played if the final had come around sooner, but the break did at least give me a chance to have treatment on the dead leg I picked up against Sheffield United.

I could, however, play golf and on our last day I played in a four-ball with our chief scout Andy King, Quinny and Bobby Saxton. I paired up with 'Kingy' and we played for a little bit of cash this time. Not that I was confident. I hadn't beaten Niall in all my time at the club while 'Sacko' was no mean player either. But things went better than expected and we ended level on the 18th hole. 'Come on, it's a nice evening so let's have a play-off down the 10th,' I said. It took some persuasion but eventually our opponents agreed.

Despite all hitting lovely drives, Kingy put his second in the rough, likewise Quinny, while I played a beauty just off of the green. Sacko, meanwhile, had put his shot in the bunker. Me and Kingy were jumping around, the money was ours. Or so we thought.

The three of us waited on the top of the green while Sacko took his shot. He hadn't played a decent bunker shot all day and I was thinking of the £100 which would be ours. We saw a couple of practice swings and whether Bobby connected, we'll never know. But then all a sudden the ball has come flying out and I could tell it was going close. It did, in fact, land six inches from the pin but then it spun back a couple more inches leaving Bobby with the simplest of putts. This was too good to be true. Surely he just threw the ball out. Anyway, he came out of the bunker saying 'Where is it? How did I do?' and when he saw the result he went mad. I couldn't believe it and all the pressure was then back on me. And I cracked, big time. My putt was pathetic and ended up ten feet from the hole. We had lost the cash and I was getting stick from my team-mate as well as my opponents. 'You tosser' was all Kingy could say as we turned in for the night.

Here I am, aged two, with my Dad Ray. I had more hair then than I do now!

Lifting the Gothia Cup on tour in Sweden as a 13-year-old. Proof that Southampton do sometimes win trophies…

Playing at the Nou Camp in Barcelona, which seemed a million miles away as a kid. Could it happen with Southampton?

Above: My first taste of the big time. Leading out Southampton as mascot against QPR in 1985.

Right: Catch of the Day. There was more to life than football, you know!

Happier times with Chris Nicholl. Mum and Dad look on as I sign my apprenticeship forms for Saints in 1990.

My professional dreams are put on hold as I line up for this Baldock Town team photo (front row, second right).

THE TEAMS AND OFFICIALS.

BALDOCK TOWN

Red/White Shirts,
Red Shorts,
Red Socks.

1. Jimmy JONES,
2. Marcelle BRUCE,
3. Ray KILBY,
4. Lawrence CULLUM,
5. Paul BOWGETT,
6. Paddy STANTON,
7. Kevin PHILLIPS,
8. Darren FENTON,
9. Lee GRAVES,
10. Danny HOWELL,
11. Steve COOK,
12. Giles PARNWELL,
14. Richard CHATTOE,
GK. Lee BOZIER.

ASHFORD TOWN

Green/White Shirt,
White Shorts,
Green Socks.

1. Joe RADFORD,
2. Andy MORRIS,
3. Adrian LEMOINE,
4. Andy PEARSON,
5. Ricky PEARSON,
6. Malcolm SMITH,
7. Jason WHEELER,
8. Nicky DENT,
9. Dave ARTER,
10. Mark STNTON,
11. Jeff ROSS,
12. Paul CARLTON,
14. Barry AGER,
GK. -.

THE OFFICIALS

The Referee   G.J. Osman (Thame, Oxon)

The Linesmen   I. MacAllister, RED TRIM, (Bishops Stortford)
               G.J. Davis, YELLOW TRIM, (Harlow)

Our line-up for the visit of Ashford Town in October 1994. I had to settle for the number seven shirt in those days.

Above: Get stuck in! I had many happy days at Watford, including the night champions Blackburn came to town in the Coca-Cola Cup.

Left: Air Phillips! It's time for lift off as I get the better of Alan Rogers to head the opener for Sunderland against Nottingham Forest in November 1997.

Above: Going up? It was a tense time for fans and players alike as we went into the 1997-98 Wembley play-off final against Charlton.

Left: I scored my best goal of the season at the County Ground but it wasn't enough as we were pipped to automatic promotion by Middlesbrough.

I'll never forget this game at Man City in January 1998 – the day I became the first Sunderland player since Bobby Gurney to score in seven consecutive games.

One reason why I'm so happy at Sunderland is the passion and support of our wonderful fans.

Back in the old routine. I put us back on the road to the Premiership with a penalty on the opening day of the 1998-99 season versus QPR.

...And finishing off the job. I tuck away a penalty – one of four goals I would score – in our 5-2 rout of Bury. After two seasons of sweat and toil, we had finally made it.

The Roker Roar. I never knew football fans could be so vocal and fanatical until I came to the north east.

The talk throughout the break was how we could combat Charlton, who had put together a fine end-of-season run to finish fourth. They were, in fact, one of the few teams we failed to beat that season and were big and strong in every department. Our game plan was to get at their defenders early and try to unsettle them. We were always confident of scoring goals, so our emphasis was clearly on attack and we worked on plenty of set-pieces that week.

With the game on the Bank Holiday Monday, we flew down to Heathrow the day before and stayed at the Hanbury Manor Hotel in Hertfordshire. It's the venue where Gazza got married and I had watched a PGA tour event there the year before. If only the club had told me we were staying there, I would have brought my clubs down from Manchester! Not that I would have been allowed to play. The mood was serious in the camp now. There was no time for fun and games, we had a job to do.

That night I struggled to sleep, although that's par for the course for me. My mind is always on the forthcoming game and I'm always given a light sleeping tablet to help me doze off. But with so much at stake, I was fighting the medicine even more this time. I emerged from the hotel at 10 am the following morning and once I'd had a light breakfast of cereal and toast, I went for a walk on my own around the golf course.

There was so much at stake that I had to be by myself to get my head together. As this was my first Wembley appearance I wanted to make sure that I had a good game because you never know when you'll be back again. Then there was another of Brian Clough's goalscoring records to go for. I knew that if I scored, I would have 35 goals and pass Sunderland's post-war record for goals in a season. Oh, and there was the small matter of promotion if we won.

It couldn't get any bigger than this, but I just had to stay focused and play my normal game. That's what I kept saying to myself all day – just treat this like any other league game. But at times, that was easier said than done.

At midday, it was time to leave the hotel. And just like a Cup final, we put on our club suits and boarded the coach. I'd had my hair shaved really short at the hotel because I knew that it would be warm and we really looked the part in our new threads. The only snag was that our shirts were light blue and it was a hot, sunny day. Within minutes everybody had big sweat patches under their arms! That broke the ice and the tension and we were soon having bets on to see who would have the biggest patches by the time we reached Wembley Way. I'm sure it was Jody Craddock who ran out the winner. His sweat stains had reached down to his belt by the time we got off the coach!

This was a whole new experience and I think only Niall Quinn and Lee Clark had played at Wembley before. On the way down to the stadium, Quinny just said to me to go out and enjoy the occasion because it would soon become a blur. There had been a lot of talk in the papers leading up to the game that my sister Karen had beaten me to Wembley by playing there for Berkhamsted Ladies. She didn't give me any Quinny-style words of advice but, with all respect, this was going to be different, much different.

You could sense we were approaching Wembley as the number of red shirts, both Sunderland and Charlton fans, started to increase. The customary airship was now in sight and the adrenalin started to pump around my body. Then it hit us, Wembley Way.

If the sight of our fans outside the Stadium of Light prior to the Ajax game was something to remember, then this was twice as breathtaking. The entire route to the stadium was awash with red shirts, even the grass banks leading up to the turnstiles.

The fact that it was a sunny day also added to the occasion and as we got nearer, our fans were singing and chanting, while the Charlton fans just looked on, waiting to see their team. It was just a shame that I didn't bring a camera with me.

Speaking to my Mum afterwards, she said the atmosphere among the fans was just as incredible. The chants of 'Super Kev' were much in evidence as she approached the stadium, although I didn't ask her whether she joined in.

The coach reversed into the tunnel and unlike at the Stadium of Light, the dressing room was unusually quiet. It had sunk in to all of us just how big a game this was. I could sense the nerves of a few of the younger lads but people like Kevin, Niall, the gaffer and Bobby Saxton were trying their best to keep us calm.

The dressing room was just as I remembered it, a vast place, the only difference being a small bar in the corner of our room and a man serving us drinks. Oh, and there was one other difference this time, it was my shirt that was hanging up and it was me who would be playing.

Once we'd dropped off our kit bags, it was time to go for the pre-match walkabout. I was one of the last onto the pitch and as I started to walk up the tunnel, all I could see were the Charlton fans at the other end. But as I broke through into the sunlight, I felt surrounded by friends. The cheers of 'Super Kev' went up and it gave me pins and needles. It's something you can't really explain unless you've been in that situation before. It really was unbelievable.

I just wanted to get on with the game now, the hype was becoming unbearable and it wasn't finished yet. Later as we were about to go back after our warm-up, I was ushered towards the centre-circle to pick up the Nationwide Player of the Year trophy from Sunderland fan and former athlete Steve Cram. I knew that I would be picking the trophy up at some point, but I didn't know that it would be in the middle of the Wembley pitch and live on TV.

The stadium was, by now, almost full. On one side I was being cheered, on the other, booed. It was a proud moment for me, to be nominated the best player in all three divisions and if someone had said 10 months earlier that I'd win the award, score over 30 goals and be playing at Wembley, I'd have laughed in their face.

Unfortunately, there was no time to savour the moment. Reflection was the last thing on my mind. I had a job to do, the accolades could come later.

It was now time for the talking to stop. I'm not one for superstitions, and just got ready how I felt. Sometimes the top goes on first, other times it's my shorts. I think most of the lads are the same, although Mickey Gray always puts on his left sock before his right.

There were no last-minute team talks, there never is. Like any other game, the tactics were done on the training pitch leading up to the game. All the gaffer said to us was, 'You've all had a brilliant season and should be proud of what you've done so far. Now let's give it one last go. Let's get what we deserve.'

And with that the referee's buzzer sounded and it was time to square up to the opposition in the tunnel. There were a few handshakes with the Charlton boys but not from me. I was so focused, just determined to win.

There was no turning back, we were now making the long walk up the tunnel for the final time and again it was the Charlton fans who were visible first. We then walked out and it was a cauldron of noise, colour and fireworks. The last thing I was expecting was the sound of huge firecrackers going off in my ears. It almost scared me to death.

As you walk onto the Wembley turf, all you want to do is look up and find your family. You know they're proud of you, and you want to win for them as much as anyone. I also paused for a moment and thought of my Dad, who would have been looking down with pride.

It was then time to line up and shake all the dignitaries' hands. But that was a pain to be honest, this wasn't the FA Cup final, this was a play-off and all I wanted to do was get the game under way.

Just like Quinny said, I had to savour the occasion otherwise it would pass me by and that's so true. The game itself is a bit of a blur to me although I remember the sense of relief when the whistle went to start the game.

I must admit that it took me a little while to get used to the pitch. It was massive, much bigger than anything I had played on before and the grass was a little longer, too. I knew from the very first minute that there would be a few tired limbs come the end of the game and I could sense that there was the potential for a few goals in the 90 minutes.

It was also more difficult to communicate. Although the Stadium of Light is big, you can still hear the instructions from the manager, but at Wembley it is completely different. The bench is miles from the pitch and when the crowd get going, you just can't hear a word the management say. You are relying on hand signals – good and bad! – and other players to pass messages on to you.

And then there are the fans. They, too, seem a long way from the pitch and it feels like you are playing in a goldfish bowl. But it's a marvellous arena for football and although the Stadium of Light is fantastic and possibly the best in Britain, there is nothing like Wembley. If anything gives you a taste for the big time and playing for England, then it's the thought of walking onto that famous turf which does it for me.

We didn't play brilliantly in the first half and I saw very little of the ball. Charlton, on the other hand, seemed to be coping with the conditions and the bigger pitch much better.

Mind you, the pressure was off them. With the way we had been playing that season and with the sheer size of the club which Sunderland had become, we were the clear favourites. We were the ones who had built this new stadium for the Premiership and we were the ones who had finished higher – if only one place – up the table.

On the other hand, Charlton had really come from nowhere to be at Wembley. They were the plucky have-a-go heroes who had the neutrals on their side. If they went up, brilliant. But if they lost, it was no big deal. They were expected to be a Division One side anyway. In truth, they had nothing to lose and everything to gain. It was the other way round for us and it seemed to be showing.

It was no surprise to me when they took the lead through their Sunderland-born striker Clive Mendonca, who turned Jody Craddock superbly on the edge of the box before firing his shot past Lionel Perez.

I couldn't even remember us creating a chance all half and for that reason alone, I was happy to go in at the break trailing by just the one goal. 'If we can raise our game by between 15 and 20 per cent, we'll win,' said the gaffer in the changing room. 'Get us an early goal and we'll be in the driving seat.'

I can remember being shattered and wanting water. I think it was a combination of the heat and the fact that I hadn't trained that often due to my dead leg. But I knew I had to give my all. This was the most important half of football I'd ever played in.

And we responded to the call from within the dressing room by equalising just five minutes after the re-start. Nicky Summerbee was thriving on the wide open spaces of Wembley and one of his pin-point corners was met by Quinny, whose low header nestled into the back of the net.

It was party time for the 38,000 Mackems who had made the trip down and I honestly thought that we would now go from strength to strength and win the game by two or three goals.

I was even more certain of victory eight minutes later. The Charlton defence had cleared the ball and as we're all running back, Bally plays a ball back into my path and I'm onside. There's only the keeper to beat and if the ball goes in, I've done it. I've broken the record and I've got 35 goals to my name for the season. But there's a lot of work to be done yet. Charlton keeper Sasa Ilic is racing towards the ball, too. I've got to get there. I do. I've got to lob him. I do. And the ball's got to go in. But will it?

Everything then goes into slow motion. The ball is bouncing towards the goal and it feels like the crowd has gone quiet in anticipation. I'm certain that the ball is on course for a divot and will bounce wide. But then I realise that I'm playing at Wembley, the pitch is as flat as they come, there are no divots and the ball's in the back of the net.

I've done it! Get in there! My head's in my hands, I look to the sky, I can't believe what I've done. It feels like I've scored the winner already.

When I look back on my career I'm sure that goal will be up in the top three. To score at Wembley is every schoolboy's dream. But it had so much more significance for me. I knew I could score goals but never in a million years did I think I could hit 35 goals and in the First Division at that.

But to be honest, I was finding this division easier than Division Two and certainly easier than when I was playing non league for Baldock. I was given far more respect at this level, players were not diving in quickly. There was too much at stake for an early bath. And I was responding to it. Of course you've got to have good team-mates, too and you've got to have ability yourself, but as the season went on I was finding it easier and easier.

When that goal went in, I had proved once and for all that I was established. And I could do it when it mattered, in the big games. For me, the First Division was finished, I had been there, scored that and bought the T-shirt. Now I just wanted to get this game out of the way and prove that I could play and score in the Premiership.

That's what went through my head and I wanted the referee to just blow his whistle and end the game as I was trotting back to the half-way line. Trouble is, there was still over half-an-hour of football to be played. And who said that football's a funny old game?

We then proceeded, not for the first time, to get the other side out of jail. We were looking comfortable for another 15 minutes and seemingly on our way to Highbury and Old Trafford when Charlton scored a carbon copy of my goal.

Instead of Kevin Ball it was Keith Jones. Instead of their back four it was ours. And instead of me it was that man Mendonca again. The score was back level at 2–2 and the balance was again turning in the Londoners' favour.

Incredibly, both teams were just hell-bent on all-out victory. Sitting back and defending never came into the equation all afternoon. With both teams looking like they would score with every attack, the defences just couldn't sit back and soak up the pressure. It just wasn't working. We looked like we would concede as many as we would score, and that's not condemning our back four because defending starts from the front, it was just one of those afternoons. It was hotting up in the stands, and on the pitch it felt as if I was playing in 100 degree heat. I was convinced that some players would also tire and there would be more goals to come.

I wasn't disappointed. Just two minutes after Mendonca had given Charlton a lifeline, Lee Clark sent in a dangerous, low cross and Quinny, obviously the man for the big occasion, ghosted in at the back post with a low shot which beat Ilic all ends up. Wembley erupted, incredibly, for a fifth time. Not that I saw much of the celebrations. Having just gone up for a header, I was in a crumpled heap on the floor. My legs had seized up with cramp and I could barely walk, let alone run. The effects of a long, hard season had finally taken their toll and the fact that I had not trained that often leading up to the final hadn't helped. So my Wembley dream was over. Just to walk out onto the turf, let alone play was a dream come true. And then to score my 35th goal, well I couldn't really ask for much more. I had mixed emotions when I was substituted for Danny Dichio. I knew I had done myself justice and was delighted that the team were winning. But I wanted to savour the occasion for as long as I could. I wanted to see the job through to the end.

I felt sorry for 'Deech'. He had come on in my place, and having arrived earlier in the season from Sampdoria, was still finding his feet at Sunderland. With Quinny and myself the first-choice strikers, he had found his chances limited to the subs' bench and it's always difficult to make an impression when you come on with just 15 minutes of a game to go.

At Wembley, he had only been on the pitch for a couple of minutes when he had a great chance to kill the game off. With time and space on his side he chose to volley the ball home instead of stooping to head it, and completely fluffed his shot. That would have been it, 4–2 and game over. Instead, Charlton had been given another lifeline. And all I kept thinking was 'If that was me, I would have put the ball in the back of the net.'

I know for a fact that poor Danny didn't sleep for a whole week after the game, reliving the moment over and over again in his head. But he's a good player and his time would come.

I just knew at that point that we were a long way from the winning post. Although I was praying that we would hold out, I just knew that Charlton would equalise. And Lionel chose the 86th minute at Wembley to drop his only real clanger of the season.

He had been in brilliant form all season and the fans had grown to love him. The save he made against Sheffield United was just one of many that helped us win games instead of drawing or losing them.

So I don't know what happened against Charlton, but he had a rush of blood and came flying out to meet a John Robinson cross, but got nowhere near the ball, taking out a couple of our defenders along the way. The ball fell to Richard Rufus, who had no trouble heading it in an empty net. He had never scored a goal in his life for Charlton and it was then that you wonder whether it's going to be your day.

It felt as if defeat had been snatched from the jaws of victory – another sucker punch which we had to take in the groin. But we hadn't lost, it was 3–3 and I remember the gaffer trying to hit this point home to all the players. I tried my best but could hardly make the touchline, such was the pain I was in.

Somehow, we managed to launch one last major push, hoping to end the game once and for all and it was no surprise that Nicky Summerbee was involved with our fourth goal of the game. He really had taken to the wide open spaces of Wembley and was causing Charlton all manner of problems that afternoon. But instead of loading the trigger, he was firing the gun this time as he met Quinny's knock down on the edge of the box first time and the ball flew into the back of the net.

I couldn't take in what was going on and it was hard to even keep track of the scoreline. We had scored four times. Surely, if you score that many goals at Wembley, you will emerge victorious?

But there was strange hush which descended over the stadium from our fans when the goal went in. Of course, they were delighted we had scored, but you could sense that they were more concerned about us throwing the lead away again, than actually celebrating the goal.

Naturally, Charlton did score. Mendonca completed his hat-trick from close range and the scoreboard showed that 104 minutes had now passed. Enough was enough. Nobody, either on the pitch or in the stands could take much more of this. I, for one, had never felt so many contrasting emotions in one afternoon of football.

And it didn't stop there. Both teams had, by now, settled for the lottery of a penalty shoot-out. There was nothing left in the tank to try and score again. The lads were absolutely shattered. They looked drained, worried and pumped up, all in one. It was unbelievable to think that nine months of hard work would be settled by seven spot kicks.

We hadn't planned for this outcome, so the gaffer was walking around the centre-circle, asking for volunteers. If I had been on the pitch, of course I would have stepped forward, but at this moment in time, with so much at stake, I was pleased to be out of the running. Who would want to miss and condemn his team-mates to another season in Division One?

What was to follow just typified what had gone before. Every spot kick hit the back of the net. The first six who had been nominated had done their job, now it was the turn of the reluctants.

Charlton had, incredibly, kept their cool and their 100 per cent record in front of goal. Someone had to miss and it was now Mickey Gray's turn. You could tell in his body language that he wasn't in the most confident frame of mind but full credit to him, he had the balls to step up and take one.

He opted for Ilic's left, the keeper guessed right and the game was over in an instant. The Charlton bench ran onto the pitch to mob their hero while we looked at each other in total disbelief and utter dejection.

Our immediate thoughts were with Mickey. How

must he be feeling? And as a local lad with red and white coursing through his veins, it must have hurt even more. Full credit to the manager, he immediately ran towards him and gave him a massive hug. That sums up Peter Reid, and the bond that exists between us all.

It was impossible to lift Mickey's head from the turf but once we'd tried, the reality of the scoreline began to sink in. It would be Charlton back in the big time next season while we would be trying to add to our wins at Prenton Park and hoping that Norwich wouldn't do the double over us again.

It didn't take us long to trudge back to the dressing room, the last thing we wanted to do was see Charlton celebrating. Once we'd got back inside, you could have heard a pin drop. Silence, apart from the odd blow of exhaustion and the odd sniffle from a tearful face. It almost felt as if someone we knew had just died.

Many of the lads had towels over their heads, including Mickey, who sat in the corner inconsolable. Personally, I felt sick to the stomach but I just didn't feel like crying. Maybe I had already felt so many ups and downs in my life that I was used to this feeling by now. All I wanted to do was get showered, changed and out of the stadium. Wembley is no place for losers and it's sad when you want to get out of the place as quick as you can.

Once we'd all started to get changed, the gaffer said his bit. 'You've done me proud,' he said. 'You've all contributed to making this a memorable season and we'll come back better for it. Next season we'll give it another go and next season we'll go one better.' His words were true enough but at that precise moment, I just couldn't think that far ahead. A year in football can be a very long time.

As I opened the changing room door, the press immediately swarmed around me. Having broken the record, I was big news but all I kept getting was 'Kev, are you staying?' and 'Will you be playing in the Premiership anyway next season?' I couldn't believe it. We'd just lost a massive game and were physically and mentally shattered but all I'm being asked about is my future at the club. There was no way I was leaving after what had happened that afternoon and, indeed, all season. We still had a job to do together and there was nowhere I would rather be playing my football.

Once I'd put their minds at rest, it was then back up to the players' lounge to see family and friends. It's quite a walk from the dressing rooms and I kept thinking about the game. Not only did I feel despair, but also frustration. Again, I just kept thinking 'how could we score four goals and lose?' The defence were inevitably blamed in the press afterwards but at the end of the day, we had kids in there: Darren Holloway, Darren Williams and Jody Craddock, who were all still learning their trade. They would hold their hands up and say that they didn't have the best of afternoons, but I would never slaughter them. After all, they were the players who had got us this far and had been superb all season long. We all had to take a share of the blame.

Not surprisingly, we didn't hang around that long. The team headed straight back to the north east, but I headed home to Stevenage as I was flying to Cyprus the very next day. Apparently, the mood on the coach was still one of complete desolation for the first hour but once a few beers had kicked in, the atmosphere soon began to change. The lads stopped off in Northampton to continue their 'wake' and the general consensus by now was 'we can't do anything about the result, so let's enjoy ourselves!'

I don't think the coach got back into Sunderland until 3 am and apparently there were a few hangovers being nursed the next day. But the players and the boss had made a pact that we would come back fighting even harder next season. We would get back to where we really belonged.

Like the rest of the squad, I let the alcohol ease my disappointment. Back in Stevenage, I got something of a hero's welcome, and that made me feel proud. But just as I approached the bar, I looked up and the game was being replayed on the TV. It was also close to the re-run of the penalty shoot-out so I kindly asked the landlord to turn the TV off.

Everything was happening so quickly that I couldn't really take the day's events in properly. In fact, it wasn't until I was lying on the beach in Cyprus that I fully realised the extent of the defeat. I was reading the *Sun* and they had printed the 1998/99 fixture list. Charlton were playing Manchester United and Arsenal in the first month, while we would be playing Swindon and QPR. It was the first time in my life that I'd sat on a beach and felt depressed.

To this day I can't bear to watch the game. I've got the Sunderland highlights video and once I've seen myself scoring at Wembley, the machine is switched off. It's just too painful. I can only think how bad it must be for poor Mickey Gray. Within weeks of the game he had received hundreds of goodwill messages from the fans and I knew that he was too much of a class player to let it permanently scar him. He would prove the following season just how good a player he was.

I still agree that the play-offs are a good thing. It keeps the season alive for so many teams and with a trip to Wembley on offer for the finalists, it usually makes for an exciting climax to the season. All you have to do is make sure that you don't finish third. It's the kiss of death for so many teams. We suffered and fourth-placed Charlton went up. Ipswich suffered a similar fate when my old team Watford, who had finished sixth, returned to the top-flight.

I'm not sure Mickey, or many of our fans will agree with me, but I also think that the penalty shoot-out is the best way of settling the game after extra-time. They say that the 'Golden Goal' is a better option but that just makes for a more defensive game because teams are just so petrified of losing.

My only reservation is the timing of the game. The final should take place as close to the semi-final as possible. I know that the league has to think about the ticket allocation, printing programmes and sorting out staff, but the players should also be thought about in these situations. At the end of the day, we are the ones who will play the game and who will ultimately decide our club's destiny.

But that was it for another year. Charlton were up and good luck to them. Deep down I knew that they would find it tough. They haven't got the biggest resources in the world and you always need to spend big in the Premiership.

Like a lot of teams that get promoted, they had good early results and even led the top flight at one point, but as the grim reality of the Premiership set in over Christmas, they began to struggle. I must admit that I watched them quite closely on TV in the top-flight, just to see how they were getting on, and it seemed to me that although they were not getting thrashed by teams, they weren't taking the chances which they had created. I don't think they were helped by the fact that Clive Mendonca missed a lot of the season out injured and they couldn't take advantage of their home fixtures. They were to be relegated on the final day of the 1998/99 season but having watched them over the course of the campaign, I knew what I would have to do, and indeed what Sunderland would have to do, if we were to take their place.

Looking back, the match at Wembley was one of the longest days of my life, but the one thing that stuck in the memory more than anything else were a few words of wisdom from Niall Quinn.

Like the gaffer and Kevin Ball, he was the one trying to console everyone at the final whistle and when we were back in the dressing room, he said to me: 'I honestly think that it's not such a bad thing for us to spend another season in Division One. It will give us all another season together, to get more used to one another. And it will give the younger lads another year's experience before they take on the Premiership.

Believe me, the Premiership is no place to be learning your trade if you're struggling every week. Maybe it's for the best.'

When you look at what's happened to Charlton, then his words are spot on. We were still quite an inexperienced bunch and I include myself in that, too. From our entire squad, I think only Quinny, Kevin, Lee Clark and Nick Summerbee had been regulars in the top-flight before. Another season in Division One would help us in our ultimate aim. But one thing was for certain; we had no other choice.

CHAPTER SIX

Golden Boots, Broken Toes

'Forget about last season, forget about Wembley. Let's go for it this time. Let's win the league,' said Peter Reid as we met up again after our summer break. Having huddled us round in a group on the training ground on the very first morning, that was all that was said. That was all that needed to be said.

The play-offs were already a distant memory by the time we had got the balls out and had got to work. The word 'Charlton' had been banned and everybody knew the task in hand now. Promotion. Nothing else entered our heads. We were clear favourites to win the First Division this time and we didn't want it any other way.

Forget the play-offs, we wanted to go up as champions this time and from those early days in July 1998, you could sense that the lads had come back a far more determined and focused outfit.

I had an extra spring in my step, having been given a new, improved contract which I was only too pleased to accept. It was a four-year deal which finally ended all the speculation surrounding my future at the club. I was happy and settled at Sunderland, playing the best football of my life and in a team which I believed would be playing in the Premiership before too long. I was also playing in a stadium and in front of fans which you'd find hard to better anywhere in the country, so why move?

I had heard through the grapevine that West Ham and Arsenal were interested but at this stage of my career I was happy. I wanted to stay at Sunderland.

Having had the best season of my life, I more than paid back my transfer fee and was rewarded accordingly. The management had obviously heard of the interest of other clubs and moved quickly to make sure that I remained a Sunderland player. That again showed the faith they had in me but I now had a bit more power to flex my muscles. The deal was an amicable one for all concerned.

The new contract meant financial security and having been unsettled in Brancepeth for some time now, I could now move on. With a few more quid in the pocket, I could afford to splash out and have a house built in a more peaceful location. For the first time in my life, I didn't have to worry too much about money and although I'm still relatively careful, it's nice to be in a position where I can buy a new house or a new car. After all, you only live once and that's something that was brought home to me the day my Dad died.

Trouble is, houses take time to build and having already agreed to rent out our current property, we were on the verge of being homeless. A professional footballer, out on the streets!

Thank goodness for Alex Rae. His neighbour owned a farmhouse, which had been unoccupied since his mother died and we were only too happy to move in. The old lady only lived in a couple of rooms and the place hadn't been decorated for 25 years. It was in a bit of a state to be honest, so in came the industrial cleaners and decorators. But we grew to love the old place, it was two miles off the beaten track and all we had for company after dark were owls and bats. The first couple of nights were eerie but we were just grateful to have somewhere to live. I could now concentrate on my football again.

What the new contract did prove to me was just how far I had come at Sunderland. If I turned the clock back one year, I was a relative unknown trying to make the quantum leap from struggling Second Division Watford to a team which had lofty ambitions to be one of the leading forces in the country. But I had succeeded, I had scored the goals which the club were desperately crying out for and I had made an impression on everyone at Sunderland. I was now a big part of the club and I could even chat to Niall Quinn without getting nervous!

But that's not to say that I was content with life. There was a lot to achieve and having missed most of the previous campaign's pre-season training due to the transfer, I was now looking forward to getting myself really fit in time for the big kick-off against Queens Park Rangers on 8 August.

Thankfully, I'm not a person who puts on weight and even when I suffered my long-term injury at Watford, I only put on a couple of pounds during that time. In fact, when the season comes to a close, I usually pig out for a couple of weeks and have a few beers, especially if I'm on holiday. But as the days and weeks pass, I'll start to get myself back in shape by going out for a few runs in the countryside. More fruit and vegetables are added to my diet and by the time of our return at the start of July, I don't usually feel too bad.

On this occasion, I made sure that I was ready. With it being my first full pre-season with Sunderland, I was expecting the boss and Bobby Saxton to put us through plenty of hard running, hill treks, cycling and weights. Although I don't put on the pounds, it doesn't mean that I'm good at pre-season training and a naturally fit person, so I was a little anxious, to be honest.

But if I was expecting a hard slog, what I found was the complete opposite. It was very relaxed, very enjoyable, with the emphasis being on ball work more than anything else.

That first week we all split up into groups of five or six teams, with five or six players within that team. And from then on, we were set tasks and a number of skills competitions for the entire five days. First we'd work on dribbling, then it would be passing and then it would be running and everything was timed by our coaches. The team which finished with the quickest time at the end of the week won a little bit of money and although it was hard work, it was stimulating, enjoyable and kept everyone on their toes. Pre-season is hated by many footballers, especially with the thought of long-distance running for days on end but this was enjoyable. Just another example of how the club has started to lead the way.

That's not to say that there was no running involved. I have to admit that I'm not that hot when it comes to endurance running during the summer months and you can usually find me towards the back of the pack, while ultra-fit Mickey Gray is leading the way at the front.

We had one particularly long running session and Gerry Harrison, whom we'd signed from Burnley, was struggling badly. We had to run four laps of our training ground and it was timed and although I was near the back, poor Gerry was still half a lap behind the last person and the manager was giving him plenty of grief. 'Come on, you lazy bastard!' was all you could hear and Gerry was blowing, badly. We had all finished and were sitting on the grass by the time he had crossed the line and he was getting abused by everyone. It's not that he was that out of condition, he just didn't look fit.

As a punishment, the gaffer left him behind while the rest of us went on our pre-season tour of the West Country. He had a week to sort himself out, or he would be in trouble.

But things did not improve for poor Gerry and we discovered a couple of months later that he had been feeling so tired because he had contracted Hepatitis B. It was no laughing matter then and he never regained his place in the side. He has since left the club and it just goes to show that even if you're a super-fit footballer, you're not invincible.

The second week of pre-season was spent on brushing up on working more as a team unit, and that's when we'd play keep ball and split up for shooting practice, while the defenders and keepers were worked separately. Then it was off to Nigel Mansell's golf and country club where we stayed while we played a number of low-key friendlies. We mixed a bit of golfing with the football and it was the ideal setting for our preparations.

There would be no Ajax this year, it was strictly low key because we just wanted to get on with things this season with the minimum of fuss. Our first game was against Plymouth and our new centre-half Paul Butler got off to the ideal start with a goal in a comfortable 3–0 win.

We then played non-league Weymouth and beat them by the same scoreline, while we completed our tour of the West Country with a hard-fought 2–1 win at Yeovil.

Again, I was amazed by the support we brought to these games, even against non-league opposition. It was incredible and we were attracting almost 3,000 for both the Weymouth and Yeovil fixtures.

Unfortunately, I was not hitting the target at this stage but I was very impressed with Danny Dichio. He netted in every game and was giving only good impressions back to the manager that he meant business this season.

We also played Manchester City in Ian Brightwell's testimonial game at Maine Road which ended goalless, but the team remained unbeaten and we were looking sharp and focused.

To be honest, it was easy just to slip back into action during the pre-season and apart from a couple of new faces, the team was the same as the one which left the field at Wembley.

The main difference was in goal. Lionel Perez had left the club, which surprised me because he had a good season. I found out when I read the papers on holiday and what surprised me even more was the fact that he had joined Newcastle on a free transfer. If the fans loved him before, I'm not sure they'll think so highly of him now!

In his place came a young Danish lad by the name of Thomas Sorensen, who had come highly recommended by Peter Schmeichel. And from the first moment I saw him in training, I knew that he was something special. In my eyes, he was better than Perez and looked like having the potential to outshine Schmeichel, too.

Also coming into the side was a big, strapping centre-half, Paul Butler. His £1.5 million move from Bury surprised me because even though I had apparently played against him twice the previous season, I couldn't remember him at all. Sorry about that, Paul.

And I was still not sure of his credentials at the start of the season, just like the Sunderland lads must have thought about me when I arrived. Having come from a side playing in front of 5,000 fans, he was now at the Stadium of Light and performing in front of 40,000 screaming Mackems. It took him a little while to settle but he went on to prove himself as an outstanding defender, a 'rock', and he soon built up a great understanding with his partner Andy Melville, himself frozen out the previous season but who came in as a replacement for the injured Jody Craddock.

I was not too surprised when the gaffer brought in a centre-half. It was clear from the Wembley game that we needed a little bit more experience in front of the goalkeeper. And no disrespect to Darren Williams, who had been playing there, but he'll be the first to admit that centre-back is not his favourite position. Little else needed tweaking and as we went into our final warm-up game at Hartlepool; we fielded the side which would take on Rangers in the Stadium of Light.

By now I was feeling fit, strong and ready for the new season. The game itself went well, we stayed unbeaten, winning 2–1 and I managed to break my duck at last.

We were now ready for league action. We had to get off to a much better start than we did the previous season, which ultimately cost us our chance of promotion.

Nothing other than victory would be good enough for the fans or the players. We had to send out a clear, early message that we meant business because the First Division would again be a tough league to break free from.

I saw our main threat coming from Ipswich and relegated Bolton, although I thought Wolves, Birmingham and Crystal Palace would also be in with a shout of going up. I was to prove myself correct, with only cash-strapped Palace falling by the wayside.

I had also set myself the target of 20 goals for the season although this time, if anyone could score 25 goals by Christmas, they would win a Mazda MX5. Quinny and myself posed for the promotional picture for the launch of the competition and I said to Quinny: 'In this team, anything is possible'. I honestly thought that with the team I was playing in, I could score that many goals, just as long as I kept myself injury free and had big Niall as my partner.

Like many teams who had come to the Stadium of Light, QPR came to frustrate us. They packed as many players behind the ball as possible and tried to hit us on the break. No matter how hard we tried, we just couldn't break them down.

We continued to play the same way we had done the previous campaign, by getting the ball out wide and putting in early crosses for Quinny and myself to get on the end of. On the left, Mickey and Johnno were giving us plenty of ammunition, while Nicky Summerbee was, yet again, putting in some superb balls. I honestly believe he is the best crosser of a ball in the country, up there with David Beckham.

But we weren't getting the rub of the green. It looked as if we would start off on a bad note again and the natives were getting restless until Darren Williams tried his luck and the ball came off their defender Ian Barrowclough's hand. The crowd instantly appealed, the referee pointed to the spot and I prepared to take the spot kick which I had missed out on a few weeks earlier at Wembley.

The decision was a harsh one if you're a QPR fan, not that I was complaining. I then hit one of my best penalties ever and drove the ball low and hard into the bottom corner of the net. The game was won with 15 minutes to go and you could sense the relief around the stadium. If we hadn't won, we might not have had the platform on which to go from strength to strength. And for me, it was important to get my name on the scoresheet again. I'm sure there were a few critics waiting for me to slip, wondering whether I was just a one-season wonder. But I had continued where I had left off. It was now time to get on with the rest of the season.

Lee Clark had been carried off during the game and when we found out afterwards that he had broken his leg, the euphoria of winning came to an abrupt end. Lee had been an inspiration to us the previous season and although his move from Newcastle was controversial, he didn't let it affect him and went on to show the entire First Division that he was playing in the wrong league.

Kevin Ball is our Captain Courageous in midfield and wins every ball he goes for, but Clarky provides the subtle touches and slide-rule passes which, as a striker, I thrive on. When we heard that he would be out for a minimum of six weeks, my heart sank. I honestly thought we would struggle without him.

I should have known better. I was forgetting about our tremendous team spirit and strength in depth. In came Alex Rae as his replacement and he went on to have an inspirational spell in the side. I have always rated Alex, from the days when he was playing for Millwall and I was at Watford, and he didn't let anyone down. Although he's since had his off-field problems and injuries, he deserves as much success as anyone at the club.

Amazingly, the season was only a game old when we were back on the Wembley trail in the Worthington Cup at York. With Quinny out with a knock, Danny Dichio was back in the side and he put in a really confident performance as he staked a claim for a first-team place. His pre-season form had continued and he scored both his goals in the first 30 minutes. The second was a cracker, an overhead kick and I was delighted for him because he had been getting a lot of stick from the fans and the press. With a run in the side, I knew he would make them eat their words.

Without sounding big headed, I had nothing to prove when it came to scoring goals but I still wanted to get on the scoresheet in open play and I felt as if I would score in our next away game at Swindon, scene of my best goal for the club.

Again, I scored another good goal which must rank in my favourite five Sunderland strikes. Having gone behind to an Iffy Onuora strike after four minutes, I scored our equaliser with a curling effort from the edge of the box on the hour. Unfortunately, we couldn't add to our tally and drew the game 1–1, but Swindon is never an easy place to go and get a result and we would have probably settled for a draw beforehand.

The game was also significant for the withdrawal of Niall Quinn with a hamstring injury. It's always a major blow to lose a player of Quinny's presence, but the good thing was that Deech was flying and couldn't wait for his league chance.

After the game, only a few of the lads opted to take the long trip back to the north east on the coach. The gaffer certainly wasn't present and with a long trek ahead of us, it was off to the back where the fridge was and the beer soon began to flow. As you can imagine, four hours later and Deech, Luke Weaver, Michael Holland and myself were having a right old party.

The music was going and we were dancing away and all of a sudden, Luke's falling straight down the emergency exit steps at the back of the coach. Amazingly, he's managed to keep his beer can in hand and hasn't spilt a drop. Not only that, he's carried on dancing as if nothing's happened. With Newcastle using the coach the following week, we naturally tidied up the mess behind us and made sure everything was perfect for them. It's just a good job we don't have many trips as long as the Swindon one every week or I'm sure the coach driver would have second thoughts about taking us!

But, again, we showed the great morale we've got in the side. Without it, I don't think we'd be as good a side.

Our target was to win four of our first six games and going into the game with Watford on 25 August, we were ahead of schedule. The draw at Swindon was the only blot as we went on to win our second leg against York, 2–1, a game where I scored from all of six yards from a John Mullins cross.

We had sent out our biggest warning yet with a 5–0 thumping of Tranmere, to record our biggest victory at the Stadium of Light. I kept my run going when I scored from a Dichio cross after 17 minutes and the amazing fact was that we won the game with seven recognised first-team players out injured.

This season would turn out to be just as much about our squad as our first XI and everything had fallen into place from the start this time. There would be no need for a police escort from the ground, no need for teas to fly out of windows, we could have even taken down our canopy at the stadium if we really wanted to.

I was looking forward to the game against Watford from the moment the fixture list was published, the visit of my old team-mates. It was no surprise to me that Graham Taylor had guided them to the Second Division title the previous season and they had started this campaign with a bang, too. This was to be a top-of-the-table clash and it was still only August.

But before I could think about the game, I was a little concerned just what kind of reception I would get from the visiting fans.

On holiday in Cyprus, I was in a bar and met a group of Watford fans and we spoke about the game and I was a little worried that things had turned sour from their point of view. But they reassured me that I would get a good reception. And I needn't have worried.

As we warmed up for the game, I received the Shoot/Adidas Golden Boot award for my 29 league goals the previous season and when I showed off the trophy to the fans, I looked up to the Watford contingent and they gave me a massive round of applause and were singing 'Super Kev' as loud as the home fans. It was a brilliant moment for me and I'll never forget it.

When it came to the game itself, I think the occasion got the better of me and I was trying too hard to score. I was trying shots from all over the pitch and it was no surprise that I finished the game without a goal to my name.

Saying that, Watford never made it easy for me and for the first half an hour, they were making it difficult for the rest of the team, too. They flew out of the blocks and went 1–0 up through Allan Smart after just 11 minutes and it took us a little time to get into our stride.

But once Johnno had equalised with one of his right-foot specials into the top corner, we soon found our feet and scored two more goals before half-time through a Nicky Summerbee free-kick and another from Deech, this time a close range header. Andy Melville went on to complete the rout in a dreary second half.

Four days later we hit the point of no return, the top of the table with a 2–0 win at Ipswich. We owed them one for last season and looked comfortable the moment John Mullins tucked home Mickey's low cross after just 11 minutes. I then picked up a ricochet from Mullins and rounded Richard Wright to score from a tight angle on the half hour and the game was safe. It was my fourth goal in five games and I felt brilliant. A one season wonder? I was having none of it.

But surely as a team we couldn't keep up this momentum, this blistering pace. We had scored 13 league goals and conceded just two. Naturally enough we 'stumbled' with back-to-back draws with Bristol City and Wolves.

Again, the Sky jinx had taken hold of us when City visited the Stadium of Light for a midweek game. We absolutely slaughtered them from start to finish and our first-half performance was the most one-sided I had ever been a part of or indeed had ever witnessed.

I had opened the scoring after just 13 minutes with a sweet left-foot volley which crashed into the top corner, but their keeper Keith Welch was having a tremendous game and stopped everything we fired at him. On another day, we could have had six or seven goals, I should have had at least a hat-trick, and he even had the audacity to save one of my penalties.

But we just couldn't add to our lead and you could sense that Bristol were going to sneak a goal at the death.

Naturally, it came from fully 30 yards out from their sub Soren Andersen and poor Thomas Sorensen, who was virtually a spectator for most of the match, just couldn't get anywhere near it. We had drawn at home but it felt like a defeat, such was our domination, but there was no way the gaffer was going to slaughter us after that. It was just one of those days.

The following game couldn't have been more different. We were on the receiving end of a roasting at Wolves and were looking dead and buried until I managed to tuck the ball home deep into injury time. We were the ones who had got out of jail this time and we celebrated like we'd won the Cup final. It was only a draw but we'd kept intact our unbeaten league record and had achieved it at Molineux, which is never an easy place to go and win.

I was also happy because I was really wound up that day. I am usually a pretty placid character on the pitch, but their defender Keith Curle was really getting to me. Now he's big and hard, which I can handle, but he's dirty with it too. There were times when an elbow went into my back or my shirt was being pulled but you just have to get on with it and hope that the referee notices. On this occasion he didn't, so it was brilliant when the goal went in. I just wanted to go up to Curle and shout 'Have some of that!'

The goals just kept on coming for me and I was voted

Sunderland Echo Player of the Month for August, not that I was entirely happy with things.

I scored six league goals in the opening seven games of the season but I wasn't playing that well. To be honest, I was being a bit lazy, the pre-season had not gone that well and I felt I was just going through the motions. The gaffer had noticed it and he told me to buck my ideas up.

We had drawn Chester City at home in the next round of the Worthington Cup, an ideal time for the gaffer to rest a couple of his more senior players and blood some of the promising youngsters at the club.

He thought it would be in my best interests to sit the game out and re-charge my batteries and although a couple of the lads took his advice, I wanted to play to show him that I was back on my game. I was on a goalscoring run which I wanted to keep going. I was still in the headlines because of my goals and I wanted the momentum to continue. I didn't feel that tired, I felt fine and I thought I could really build up my goal tally against lower league opposition.

It proved to be the biggest mistake of my career. True enough, I got on the scoresheet as we cruised to a 3–0 first leg victory, hitting our second following a lovely though ball from Alex Rae. But not long after I had scored my goal, my good start was about to hit a brick wall. Having picked the ball up on the half way line and with my back to the Chester goal, I could see out of the corner of my eye that one of their defenders was rushing towards me. Then, all of a sudden, he came flying in, stamping on my left foot in the process. I was in agony and all I could remember was our bench jumping up in fury at the challenge. It was bad, and only the bloke – whose name I can't remember – can say whether it was malicious or not. One thing's for certain, if I met him again I certainly wouldn't be buying him a beer.

I immediately knew that I had picked up a bad injury. I thought I had broken my big toe or possibly even my foot and there can be no worse injury for a footballer – they are the tools of the profession and a fracture could mean weeks on the sidelines. But as the game wore on, the pain eased up a little and the worries from within began to ease.

That evening, however, I was in absolute agony, my big toe was giving me so much pain that I didn't sleep a wink all night, so the next morning I spoke to our physio Gordon Ellis and we went for a scan.

I was expecting the worst but once the X-ray came through, nothing serious had shown up. I was told that I just had severe bruising and I'd be back in action within a couple of weeks. That was the best news I could expect to hear and I was hoping to be back playing by the end of September at the very latest.

In the meantime, I just had to put my feet up and rest. Any pressure on the foot would hinder the healing process and with an injury so small as your toe, there's no point in trying to pack it with ice.

The swelling did go down within a couple of weeks, but trying to walk was still absolute agony. This wasn't predicted by the doctors and I started to feel a little concerned. I was certain that something more serious than bruising had been inflicted but if the doctors didn't have a clue, what hope did I have?

Gordon went on to try every treatment under the sun, including ultrasound and even ice, but nothing was responding and time was getting on. The last thing I needed was a lengthy injury like the one I had picked up during my time at Watford. I wanted to be known as Kevin Phillips the striker, not Kevin Phillips the crock. Word soon gets around if you are injury prone, so I wanted to get back in action as soon as I could.

Gordon continued the extensive treatment and after another period of rest, it was time to test out the injury again. We are now talking three weeks after the challenge and I was getting anxious. It was time to see how I got on at the training ground. I could walk fairly comfortably so I was hopeful of being back on the right track. But once I'd got stripped and ready for action, I could hardly run, let alone kick a ball.

I could see in Gordon's eyes that this was serious and the manager, who had Lee Clark out as well, was getting very concerned. I was at breaking point.

The only option for me now was to see the club's specialist, Dr De Kiever, but like everyone else, he dismissed the injury as just bad bruising and was adamant that it would go away. Were all these professional men just fobbing me off? Surely not, they can't all be wrong, so I decided to put my feet up and rest for another week, while still having treatment at the club every day.

The seriousness of the injury was brought home to me when the club tried to fly me to see the world's leading foot specialist, a bloke called Dr Mann, who had operated on a number of leading sportsmen in

California. Although I was injured and concerned, I was well up for a couple of weeks in the sun on the west coast. Well, if I couldn't play football, that seemed the best place to go at the time.

Unfortunately, we couldn't tie him down to a consultancy date and as we were getting anxious ourselves, we met the top man in England, Dr Weeber, who works in Middlesbrough. Not quite the States, but if it meant that my problems would be solved, that was of far more importance.

He took me for a series of X-rays and scans but still no injury showed up. I had a foot injury which was managing to baffle the entire medical world but why did it have to happen to me, during the football season and during a time when I was on a great goalscoring run?

There was only one thing for it. I would have to be operated on to get to the root of the problem. My worst nightmare had come true. Watford revisited. Why me? Why did I play against Chester?

All I could envisage was another lengthy spell out on the sidelines, which is inevitable after surgery. For the non-professional footballer, an operation often means time off work to recuperate with feet up on the sofa, but for us it's the most frustrating time ever. You want to be playing and helping the team, but you're stuck on the sidelines, kicking every ball from the stands. You also miss out on the daily banter in the dressing room, the chats with your mates, and you often have too much time on your hands.

Once you've received treatment in the morning, you can be back home by 11 o'clock. But unlike at Watford,

I was determined to use my free time better. There would be no days spent just sitting in the pub. This time I had Millie to come home to, I had my forthcoming wedding in the summer to start preparing for and I had the new house to visit which, incidentally, was now starting to take shape.

I was just hoping that I would not be out of action for too long. Clarkey's leg was almost ready for action in a couple of months and all I had damaged was a toe. That's the hope I carried with me as I hit the operating table. Kevin Phillips would be back so soon that you would never guess that he had been away.

Then it was off to the Evelyn Hospital in Cambridge to go under the surgeon's knife. The man in question was a Dr Meggit, the only doctor in the country who had the knowledge to carry out the intricate exploratory operation which I required on my toe. I was just hoping and praying that he would find the problem, otherwise my career really would be on the line, just like it was at Watford.

I was soon drifting off into the world of deep sleep, hoping that by the time I returned, I would be well on the way to recovery and back in the red and white shirt before long.

CHAPTER SEVEN

Who Needs Phillips?

It was a bad time to be missing from action. In my absence, the team was going from strength to strength. I was not being missed at all, which was rather worrying, and the same could be said for Lee Clark and my strike partner up front, Niall Quinn.

All three of us had proved to be key members of the first team, yet our replacements were proving more than adequate. In for Clarky came Alex Rae, for me it was Michael Bridges and for Quinny it was Deech and the team was working like a machine. If one part broke down, a replacement would be found, and the machine would be just as efficient again.

That would be the scenario for the entire season. We would also lose Nicky Summerbee, Allan Johnston, Mickey Gray and Chris Makin at key moments during the campaign, but they would scarcely be missed, such was the strength in depth we now had at the club.

Of course, it was not quite on the same scale but we

could be compared in some way to Manchester United in the Premiership. Alex Ferguson knows how important a squad system is to a successful side and when the likes of Dwight Yorke and Roy Keane are missing, he can bring in players of the calibre of Teddy Sheringham and Nicky Butt. In the First Division, we clearly believed we had the strongest squad and our performances were proving it.

A 7–0 scoreline against Oxford was taking things to the extreme, however. And this was in the very next game after I had sustained my injury! Amazingly, all three replacements – Bridges, Dichio and Rae – grabbed two goals a piece to record our biggest win at the Stadium of Light and to move within one point of Huddersfield, who had been vying with us all season for the top spot.

It was a truly awesome display of attacking football and as I sat up in the Main Stand with Julie, I could not help but feel a hint of jealousy and frustration as we began to run up our cricket score. Not only that, I just knew what the press response to the game would be. 'You wait, the papers will be full of "WHO NEEDS KEVIN PHILLIPS?" headlines,' I said to Julie. And that is exactly what happened by the time Monday's papers came around and I think a couple of national papers used a headline very similar. That angered me after the goalscoring start I had made to the season, indeed to my Sunderland career, but it just made me more determined to fight back and show them that Kevin Phillips is a key part to the Sunderland success story.

I was pleased to see Chester finished off in the Cup, with another Johnno curler taking the tie 4–0 on aggregate. We then had back-to-back long distance away games at Portsmouth and Norwich, the first at Fratton Park ending 1–1 thanks to another Johnno goal and that took us to the top of the league. We failed to beat Norwich again, and had an own goal from their keeper Andy Marshall to thank for the equaliser in a 2–2 draw. More significantly, the game marked the return to action of Quinny. And he duly responded with our opening goal. To have his strength, stature and experience back in the team was like a new signing to us all.

But I was fast becoming the forgotten man of football. Although things weren't as bad as they were at Watford, where I just drifted away from the scene almost completely, it was hard for me to take, having been in the headlines all the time. The fans, too, were also starting to notice my prolonged absence, especially in the weeks leading up to the operation.

The specialists didn't have a clue what was wrong with me at this point, so the fans were just kept in the dark. But they're not stupid, they knew that the injury was a bit more serious than a bruised foot, otherwise I would have been back in action by now. And that's when the rumour mill started to turn.

When you're out injured, you still have to stay as fit as possible by coming in and doing a few leg and body weights and one morning, I'd just turned up when Michael Bridges came over to me and told me that he'd heard that I'd had a toe amputated and was wondering whether it was true. I was astonished. How could people make up such a thing when they didn't know the real truth? But that was only one rumour. It also got back to me that some people were saying that I had cancer in the toe and that my career was finished. It was incredible and it makes me laugh now, but at the time I found it all a little disturbing. And what concerned me just as much was the fact that I didn't know what was wrong either. An amputation might well have been a possibility, who knows?

I finally had the operation at the end of October, fully six weeks after the Chester game and I really felt it was make or break time when I came around following the anaesthetic.

In my eyes my season, and possibly career, were on the line and after 25 minutes of pulling and probing my left foot, Dr Meggit had found some damage, a hell of a lot of damage, in fact.

In each toe, you have pads which sit on the bone called bursars and these protect the bones. The one in my big toe had been completely crushed and small fragments were floating around in the joint. Not only that, the cartilage had come away from the bone too.

A toe joint works in exactly the same way as a knee joint and he told me that if I had injured my knee in the same way, I would have been out of action for a year. But as it was my toe, he was hopeful that I would be playing first-team football again early in the New Year.

Dr Meggit flushed out the toe and said that the bursar would heal in its own time. Much of the pain had been caused by the fragments which were floating around in the joint but now they were gone, I could get on with the business of rehabilitation without any worries in the back of my mind. I was desperate to return to football. I was missing out on so much.

It also meant our fans could at last be told the truth and I wanted them to hear it from me, not on the grapevine. It was at this time that I also started attending a number of Sunderland sportsmens' dinners in the north east area, where our fans got to find out exactly what had been happening to me over these last few worrying weeks. Kevin Ball used to represent the club but with his testimonial year in full swing, he was too busy and I was asked whether I would like take over.

I accepted because I wanted to give something back and show my appreciation of the fans, although I have to admit that it was quite nerve wracking in the early days, having to stand up and talk to a room full of blokes, some of whom were quite clearly worse for wear after an evening on the ale. It used to amaze me that I could play in front of 40,000 fans every other week, but when a hundred or so men were looking straight at me, I found it a little bit intimidating.

But as time went on, I got used to it and most of the questions I got asked were the same wherever I went. I'm just glad that I wasn't involved during the time when we got relegated or at the start of my first season at the club. Although you get a few quid for giving up your time, I would have wanted danger money back then!

As I've said, I'm a bad spectator when I'm out injured and spent quite a lot of my spare time back home in Stevenage, to be around family and friends, so I could just take my mind off of the injury and talk about other things.

But Sunderland AFC was never too far away and one Sunday lunchtime I took my Mum out for a bite to eat at my local pub and our game at West Bromwich Albion was on the TV. A win was important to keep the momentum going, the team having drawn 0–0 at home to Bradford, on the back of the stalemates at Norwich and Portsmouth. The press were wondering if we'd started to lose our way again, even though we were now 15 games unbeaten, but the lads had been really determined earlier that week in training, and I knew we would win.

When I got to the pub, I ordered a Ploughman's and sat down, with foot rested safely on a chair. At this stage, only a few people in the pub knew that I was a professional footballer, let alone a Mackem. But as the game swung backwards and forward, word had got around that Kevin Phillips was in the place.

The game itself was a tremendous spectacle although as we kicked off, I was a little worried whether we'd get all three points as we were on Sky again (remember that jinx?). And when we went two goals down by half-time, I was ready to pull the pub's satellite dish down. But I was forgetting our team spirit and when Andy Melville pulled a goal back, I could see hope. And so could those watching in the pub, judging by the noise. They were all on my side now and by the time Michael Bridges had equalised with a fantastic strike, the cheers had grown even louder.

We were now well into the game and everyone in the pub had, by now, drunk more than a couple of beers. I could just sense that we would get a third and win the game and I was worried about people jumping on my foot.

And the players didn't disappoint me. With four

minutes left on the clock, big Niall rises, flicks the ball into the path of Captain Courageous and the ball's in the back of the net. GOAL! The players erupt and this pub, 300 or so miles from Sunderland erupts at the same time. I couldn't contain myself either. All thoughts of my toe had gone and I was jumping, or rather hobbling, around the pub. It was a brilliant moment and we had buried that Sky jinx too. Never again would we have to worry about playing on a Sunday lunchtime!

The toe escaped unharmed and I was buzzing by the time I left. It almost felt like being on the terraces myself and it's amazing to think that so many people from my home-town now look out for the Sunderland result, just because I play for them. Of course, most of my mates support the likes of Arsenal, Spurs or Chelsea but it's good to know they're behind me and show an interest in my football.

That's why when I'm back home, I like to find out what they've been up to. Just because I'm a professional footballer now, doesn't mean that I've changed or gone 'big time'. I think some players fall down that path when they've got the fame and a bit of money in their pocket all of a sudden, but that's just not my style.

I know where I've come from and how hard life was for me at one point, and that makes me appreciate what I've got now. And I think that's the same for any footballer who's come into the game the same way as me. Ian Wright's probably the best example of that.

I'm lucky that I have a few quid now, but that doesn't mean that I'm a better person than anyone else. And I know that football doesn't last forever. There could well be a time when I'm not in the public eye anymore but, hopefully, I'll still have my family and friends then.

And it's then that I'd like to give something back to the game. I know that when I first went to Southampton, I loved it when I was made mascot for the day – it was just brilliant being around these players you only ever see on TV. And I'd like to coach youngsters from the schools and the clubs I played for. I want them to think 'Well, if Kevin Phillips can make it, then so can I'. Hopefully I can be a role model to them.

By November, I was now stepping up my fitness programme and the gaffer was coming into the treatment room every day to see how I was getting on. I thought that was a nice touch and he told me not to worry because as soon as I was fit, I'd be right back in contention. It was his words that spurred me on because I didn't then have the added worry of whether I'd face a big struggle to get back in the side. I knew that if I got myself fit and worked hard in training, I'd be back in the team.

Our biggest test of the season came at Huddersfield, for a clash of the top two. And although we drew the game 1–1, I sensed we were the far stronger side and that our hosts would probably fade as the season went on. We laid siege to their goal in the second half but all we had to show for it was a Kevin Ball strike. We drove away from the division's leading side feeling disappointed and that proved more than anything else that we should, and would, soon take over their mantle.

That duly came in the next game, thanks to Deech's header against Bury at the Stadium of Light and we then wouldn't look back for the rest of the season.

Grimsby took us to extra time in the Worthington Cup but Quinny's right foot shot with the minutes ticking away won us the game 2–1, which set us up nicely for a trip to Goodison Park to face Everton.

Now if we had aspirations to be a Premiership club, then this would be our first real test against one of the biggest clubs in the country. Okay, Everton were having a rough ride in the Premiership but they still had international players of the quality of Dave Watson, David Unsworth and John Collins in their side, so we knew we would be in for a tough test.

I did not travel with the team but was a studio guest on Tyne Tees for their late night highlights programme. We had a live feed for the entire match before we went on air and as the studios are based in Newcastle, I was expecting to get a rough ride from the people working behind the scenes on the show. But to my surprise, most of them were Sunderland supporters, so there was quite a good atmosphere.

We went on to put in a great performance and Michael Bridges scored our goal of the season with a shot which gave their keeper Thomas Myhre absolutely no chance. Collins equalised with one of his customary free-kicks and the game drifted towards a penalty shoot-out.

'Oh no, this is the last thing we need!' we all said in the studio. And the kicks proved to be just as nerve-wracking as the ones we'd taken six months earlier. Not surprisingly, Mickey Gray opted to sit this one out and we expertly took our penalties to run out 5–4 winners. Back in the studio we were jumping about all over the place and again proved just how good we were at playing under pressure. We had taken a Premiership scalp and were easily the better team on the night. If we could go on and get promotion, then I felt that we would have nothing to fear.

By the time the programme came on after the 'News At Ten', the match had only just finished at Goodison and I still had a massive grin on my face. I was so pleased for the lads and just as we were about to go on air, a message came over the loudspeaker. 'Er, Kevin, can you try and keep a straight face now, you've got to go on air as if you don't know what the score is yet.' What? We'd just beaten Everton and I've got to act like Mr Sensible. It was hard, especially when I was introduced at the start of the show, but I managed it, just. I was starting to become a bit of an old hand at all this TV lark.

On the league front, things were just getting better and better. One of my favourites for promotion, Bolton, were beaten 3–0 at the Reebok Stadium, although I thought we were lucky to have 11 men on the pitch for much of the game when Paul Butler took one of their men out. Crewe were also taken to the cleaners 4–1 and two goals from Martin Smith helped us to a 3–1 win against Grimsby at the Stadium of Light, which took us five points clear at the top of the table.

This was incredible. It was late November and having buried our Vale Park hoodoo we were the only team in the country to remain unbeaten, not just in the league but in the cup as well.

But all good things must come to an end and after predicting live on Soccer AM that we would beat Barnsley at home, I flew straight back up to Wearside to watch the game which we lost 3–2 despite another one of our famous fightbacks from a 2–0 deficit.

The result caused shockwaves throughout the division and as the lads sat down in the changing room, the gaffer had a good, long chat with us. 'Forget today, we had to lose sometime,' was his assessment. 'It's how we bounce back which is important. Prove to me in the next game that we can do it, show me we have the bottle and the guts, as well as the skill, to be champions.'

This was also proving to be a frustrating time for me off the football pitch, too. The lads seemed to be playing more golf than ever and I was missing out on trying to get my handicap down. But one player who also thought his golf had been put on hold was Luke Weaver. That week, a few of the younger lads decided to get away from it all with a couple of rounds of golf at the Woodham Golf Course. Somehow, they'd managed to blag their way on to the course for free but Luke took advantage and had already been warned by the greenkeeper for messing about and abusing club rules. Not that he took much notice. One of the holes has a steep bank and a lake. Luke has a buggy. It's not hard to guess what happened next. Head first into the water!

Not only that, Mr Greenkeeper was watching the lot and apparently went absolutely berserk. Luke was immediately banned and told that he would be reported to the club.

Despite pleading his innocence the following morning, Bally gave him a right roasting and told him that the gaffer had found out and that he would be severely disciplined. Of course, this was not true but it was good to see Luke sweat all morning waiting for the gaffer to pull him over, and I'm sure he won't mess about so much in the future!

On the pitch the lads responded in the best possible way at Sheffield United, with Quinny and Bridges scoring two goals each. Such was our dominance that we were 3–0 up at half-time. Again, it was hard for me watching in the stands. Both of the scorers against United and Deech were scoring goals for fun and running away from me in the goalscoring charts. I just wanted to start playing again.

I would find out when that would be possible the following week with a trip back to Cambridge to see Dr Meggit. I travelled down on the train with Gordon, but we arrived far too early for our appointment, so we went into town to find somewhere to eat. It proved to be a big mistake as by the time we had finished our meal, we were running late and then the taxi driver had taken us to the wrong hospital.

It was also rush hour in Cambridge with cars and bikes everywhere. We eventually made up on lost time and turned up at the Evelyn Hospital five minutes late but as we walked into the waiting room, there was not a spare chair to be found.

Sitting in one corner was John Collins and the Everton physio and I got chatting to them. He had suffered a similar toe injury and informed me that he'd already been waiting an hour-and-a-half to see his specialist. What? That would mean missing our train and getting home at about three o'clock in the morning. I sat back in my chair and resigned myself to a very long wait.

But only five minutes or so had passed when the nurse called out 'Mr Phillips'. I was surprised, while the look on John Collins' face was one of amazement. Apparently, while I'd been chatting to John, Gordon had gone to have a word in the nurse's ear to say that my wife was about to give birth and that I had to be back in Sunderland as soon as possible. I was in stitches, but Gordon had pulled a master stroke. We had a good laugh about it on the train journey home and it was funny to think that we had left John Collins, this Scottish international who had played for Celtic and Monaco, stuck in the waiting room while we had jumped the queue.

We also came out in a good mood because I had been given the all clear to start full training again. I knew that I was back on the road to recovery and the pair of us celebrated with a couple of glasses of bubbly on the way back.

It was now December and Luton were our next victims in the quarter-finals of the Worthington Cup, where we ran out comfortable 3–0 winners after they had a man sent off. Stockport and Crystal Palace were beaten in the league, likewise Port Vale who we beat 2–0. Martin Smith scored in that game, to take his tally to four goals in six league starts. Yet another player who was proving to be such an invaluable squad member.

The season was flying by, but I would again spend a Christmas out of action. This was getting to become a bit of a habit but it also meant that this year I would miss out on the club's Christmas paintballing day. The whole squad went down to Scotch Corner and as I've been before, I know just how painful those balls are if you get hit. And it was not to be a day Michael Holland would care to remember.

Apparently Michael's running around on his own and in the distance, Quinny's turned to Kevin Ball and said 'Bet you can't hit him from here'. Bally has turned round and said, 'Just watch me.'

He's pulled the trigger and hit Michael right in the back of the head. The poor bloke crashed to the floor in agony and the rest of the lads are joining him on the floor in stitches! The masseur had to treat himself! It sounded like a brilliant day, but at least I could join the lads for our meal and a drink in the evening.

My training was stepped up quite dramatically once all the festivities were out of the way. We had mixed fortunes, suffering our customary defeat at Tranmere on Boxing Day – only our second defeat of the season. We also drew 0–0 at Birmingham before getting back on track with a 2–0 win against Crewe.

With Clarky already back in action, it was now my turn.

Although I was getting twinges in my toe, there was no turning back and I was putting in some sprinting practice and training with the youth team in the week leading up to our Third Round FA Cup tie at Lincoln in early January.

Then after training on the Thursday, the gaffer came over, put his arm round me and said 'I'm putting you on the bench on Saturday.'

What? I was nowhere near fit and I think he knew that, but he got me kitted up, so that I could feel like I was part of the team again.

I got a great reception from the crowd when they saw

me run out for the warm-up but by the time the game had kicked off, I started to feel a little nervous. I knew that if anything happened to one of our forwards, I could be plunged back into action. It could be too soon, and it could mean damaging my toe again.

Not only was it a relief to see Gavin McCann score, which put us into round four, but it was a relief that I remained on the bench until the final whistle. 'PHILLIPS IS BACK' said the local press and I now had another seven days until our trip to QPR, a game which I was hoping to be eased back into action.

That Wednesday, we held a practice game at the training ground for the reserves against the youth team. It was quite a light-hearted affair but as the gaffer was watching me closely, I still wanted to put in a good showing.

I played for the reserves and scored from some distance. The goal meant absolutely nothing but for me, it was a wonderful feeling just to score a goal again. I was also putting myself about a bit in tackles and only feeling a slight discomfort from the injury.

The gaffer was obviously impressed with what he saw and as I went to get changed, he said 'Kev, you're starting on Saturday.'

I was obviously delighted but I thought I would be bedded in slowly, with a couple of reserve outings and a couple of substitute appearances. The gaffer had said that I would get my place back in the side but I didn't think it would be so immediate, especially as Deech and Michael had been playing so well in my absence. But I couldn't worry about them anymore. This was now about me. I was back in the team and back with the boys but it had been so long that I could hardly remember what my routine was for away games.

As I boarded the coach, it was like I had never been away. Johnno had kept my seat warm for the past four months and when we got to our base at the Royal Lancaster Hotel in London, we were room mates again.

We were back in the old routine – crashing out on our beds on arrival, ordering cheese and onion toasties and then having a quick nap before our evening meal, which is usually served at about 7.30 pm.

It was good to have Johnno around again. Like me, he is pretty quiet on away trips, which is ideal when you're trying to prepare for the big game ahead. I'm not one of these players who stays up late watching TV or listening to music. I'm already focused on the game ahead. Allan's the same and I just pray that I never have to share a room with our reserve keeper Andy Marriott. He gets loads of stick when we travel away because he just eats and eats and eats. If I ever shared with him I just know that he'd be ringing downstairs for room service every half an hour!

The following morning, I got up at about 9.00 am and, just like I did prior to our game at Wembley, I went for a walk on my own. Hyde Park was just across the road, so I went for a stroll and ended up playing the game in my mind. I just wanted an easy afternoon, no hard challenges and a goal.

Well, one out of three ain't bad.

As we went out for our warm-up, the reception I got was absolutely brilliant. Our fans had taken over Loftus Road again and it felt like a home game. But if I was hoping for an easy ride, I was very much mistaken as their big defender, Danny Maddix, was following me all over the pitch. This was not what I wanted to happen on my first game back. He was all over me like a bad rash and I just couldn't get into the game.

That was, until the 33rd minute. Gavin McCann broke down the left, swung in a hopeful cross and I was on to it in a flash. For once I'd left the big man in his traps and got to the ball first. I connected full on the volley on the outside of the boot. The connection felt sweet, the result, even sweeter.

I'd managed to guide the ball into the back of the net like a missile. Their keeper couldn't get anywhere near it and we had scored. I had scored. I couldn't believe it. The headlines in the papers had already been written and I was in a dream world. After all that time in the wilderness, I was back … and how!

I also scored right in front of our fans and the whole stand erupted. I just ran towards them in disbelief and pointed to the number 10 on the back of my shirt and kept shouting 'I'm back, I'm back!'

Yet another wonderful memory that will stay with me throughout my life, in fact the entire game is one that will not easily be forgotten.

We eventually drew 2–2. That man Maddix equalised on the stroke of half-time, just as Kevin Ball was being sent off for 'foul play' – an absolutely scandalous decision by the referee which would later get over-turned – and Quinny grabbed our equaliser deep into injury time with a strong header after Kevin Gallen had given Rangers the lead.

As the game wore on, I was feeling absolutely shattered but had to stay on the pitch after the sending off. Again, I was pushed back into midfield and I was running on nothing but adrenalin.

Although we had drawn the game, it felt to me like victory, having grabbed such a late equaliser and having scored myself. As I walked off the pitch, I saluted our fans, safe in the knowledge that I could still do it, I could still score goals despite four months out of the game.

I think I was helped by the fact that I returned to a side that was winning games and playing well. It was not like we were struggling to find the target and I was expected to just click into action and start scoring like a machine.

Although I was expecting to score, I think everyone else was just hoping that I wouldn't suffer any reaction to my injury, and that was all. But the goal soon changed their opinions. I was expected to score the goals to get us back in the Premiership. I had to be that machine.

After the game we headed to a Sunderland London Supporters' Club function in Swiss Cottage for a few drinks and I don't think I've received so many pats on the back before. The fans had laid on a good spread for us and we returned their hospitality by spending a good couple of hours with them.

Then it was off to the bright lights of the capital. Most of us ended up in the Emporium nightclub to let our hair down and I soon got chatting to Wimbledon's Efan Ekoku, who happened to be there with a few mates. He seemed genuinely interested in how I was getting on at Sunderland. To have a top Premiership star come up to me and start talking football just proved how my career

153

had progressed these past 18 months. I doubt whether Efan would have looked twice if I had still been at Watford. Mind you, I doubt whether I'd have been in somewhere like the Emporium at all. I would have been turned away at the door.

The phone started to ring again that week. I received a lot of press coverage leading up to our home clash with fellow promotion hopefuls Ipswich on the Sunday, but it was a lot of fuss about nothing.

I faded badly in the game and felt well off the pace. The strains of Division One that first game had caught up with me and my lack of match fitness was beginning to show. We won a scrappy game 2–1 but I can't remember too much about it. And it was no surprise when I was substituted.

But I needed no motivating for our next two games, an FA Cup fourth round match at Blackburn and our first leg Worthington Cup semi-final against Leicester at the Stadium of Light. Both games would see us again pitted against top-flight opposition and not only were we using them as Cup games, they were yardstick matches for the following season, should we get promoted.

The first clash was the match at Ewood Park and although we lost 1–0, we thought the scoreline flattered Rovers because we were far the better team for long spells. From a personal perspective, I'll remember the game for the clash I had with Jeff Kenna, my old digs mate at Southampton.

He came in late on me and I went sprawling. It was his second offence and he had to go. The home fans were incensed and some were saying that I dived. But I would never deliberately try to get a fellow pro sent off, especially not a former club mate, and as he ran towards the tunnel, I caught him up just to let him know that I hadn't made a meal of the challenge.

We shook hands in the bar after the game and he said how impressed he was with our performance. And who was I to argue? We conceded a poor goal, that was all, and we came away from the ground with plenty of credit. But I could see why Rovers would be relegated at the end of the season. They didn't gel at all and had too many individuals in the team, and I knew that Leicester would be a far tougher proposition.

Which proved to be the case. We wanted to sample Wembley again, but the Twin Towers seemed a million miles off after Leicester absolutely murdered us at times in the opening half. Their off-the-ball running, passing and strength gave us a better indication of what to expect in the Premiership while in Tony Cottee, they had a striker who knew exactly where the target was.

He scored two quite brilliant goals in the game, one in either half, and I was in awe of him. The gaffer gave us a bit of a roasting at half-time but in all honesty, Leicester were superb. 'There's still three quarters of this semi left to go, they won't be able to keep that up,' the gaffer kept telling us, and we responded with a much better second half showing.

We put more pressure on their keeper Kasey Keller and although we had fallen two goals behind, we were given a lifeline for the second leg when Gavin McCann's hopeful 75th minute free-kick into the box deceived everyone and ended up in the back of the net. The atmosphere in the dressing room after the game was far more positive. We knew we were still in with a shout but, ever the perfectionist, I was mad with myself for missing an early header, which I should have put away. If that had gone in, it could have been a completely different story.

The talk after the game was not of how we could still make it to Wembley but of an on-pitch bust-up surrounding Kevin Ball and Lee Clark. Just before we had scored our goal, they had an argument over who would take a free-kick and even had each other round the throat. Within minutes, Clarky had been substituted and instead of sitting in the dug out, he ran straight down the tunnel and into the showers. The press afterwards were full of stories that it was the end for Clarky and he had played his last game for the club, but nothing could have been further from the truth. These things happen from time to time when you're losing and it's part borne out of frustration, part out of a determination to win. But after the game it was forgotten about and both players shook hands.

More worrying for me was the fact that I had now gone three games without a goal and was still trying to get myself fully match fit again. But the gaffer was pleased with my contributions and he was pleased with the team, despite the two defeats.

Now it was back to league action and my return to Vicarage Road. I had spoken to Robert Page earlier that week and he told me that the game was a sell out for the first time since their old First Division heyday. That gave me a buzz of anticipation and I really wanted to put in a good showing.

It seemed really strange, going back through the main entrance and seeing a few old faces, saying 'hello' to the gateman, the ticket collector and just standing in the corridor next to the changing rooms.

But there was no more time for sentiment. I had to get myself focused on the game in hand. We needed to start winning again and I had to start scoring, but I knew the task would not be that simple.

Incredibly, Watford had continued their early-season form and were on the fringes of the play-offs. Victory for them would be a massive step in their pursuit of a place in the Premiership and they started just like they did at our place earlier in the season, again taking us by surprise.

I managed to get an early shot in on goal and, amazingly, the Watford fans started singing 'Super Kev'. And they were soon jumping about when Nick Wright gave them the lead.

We managed to pull it back to 1–1 before half-time when my shot looped up off former Sunderland keeper Alec Chamberlain and Quinny headed home the rebound. The gaffer told us to up our work rate by 10 per cent in the second half and we did just that. Unfortunately for us, Chamberlain was having a great day and was keeping everything out. And just as we were going for the kill, Watford broke up the other end and scored through Gifton Noel-Williams.

The result was hard to accept. We had lost again. Three straight defeats for the first time in my Sunderland career and the natives were getting restless. After the game I met up with a few of my old team-mates but my mind wasn't on the conversation as it should have been. I had not scored for four games and I was getting anxious. We were now entering a crucial period of the season, the big push for promotion, and the next couple of weeks would pave our destiny. It was critical that we got back to winning ways and I got back to scoring goals. That was the only thing on my mind.

CHAPTER EIGHT

Back Where We Belong

The sixth of February, nineteen ninety-nine. The start of the best period of my footballing life so far. The date marked the visit of Swindon Town and it also marked the start of a run which would send Sunderland back into the Premiership. It would also see me rediscover my goalscoring boots in a run in which I would score 16 goals and finish as the club's leading scorer again.

To prepare for the climax to the season, the gaffer took us away to the Marriott Hotel in Manchester. Again, we needed a break after three straight defeats because the atmosphere in the city was getting a little bit uneasy. The break came immediately after the Watford game, which we were pleased about because the press would have been on our case if we'd gone straight back home.

We had intended to spend three days at the Marriott relaxing, training and playing a bit of golf. Unfortunately, the Manchester weather was typically wet and the local course was underwater. But at least it gave us the chance to work on a few ideas in training and we had a bit of a clear-the-air chat with the gaffer and Sacko.

'I'm happy with what we've achieved so far, but we've got to bounce back right now just to keep the daylight between ourselves and the rest,' Peter said. 'If we do that, we can win this division.'

We all agreed, obviously, but we'd made a pact not to talk about winning championships until the job was done. We knew that this game can shoot you in the foot and anything could happen with three months of the season still to go. From a personal point of view, I was not entirely convinced that we'd walk away with things, anyway. We still had tough home games against the likes of Wolves and Bolton, while we had tricky away trips at Bradford, Bury and Stockport during the final push for promotion.

Refreshed from our break, we settled down to our home match against Swindon. At the end of 90 minutes, the feeling among the players and fans was one of sheer relief. We cruised to a 2–0 win and I had scored my flukiest goal of the season, sticking out a foot as Johnno tried a shot at goal. But I didn't care, I needed that goal so badly and the confidence was back in the dressing room. So too was the ghettoblaster. With three defeats, we hadn't had the chance to unwind to music as we dressed back into our club suits, but the tunes were

The proudest day of my footballing life. My England debut versus Hungary, 28 April 1999. Here I go head to head with their left-back Gyorgy Korsos.

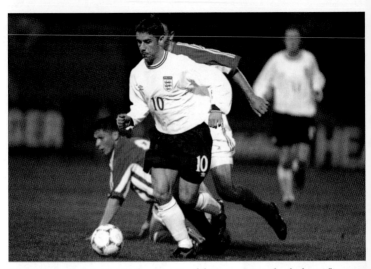

Cool, calm, collected. Despite the enormity of the game, I never let the butterflies get to me in Budapest.

Left: Cleaning Shearer's boots? That was the case in my YTS days at Southampton, but against the Hungarians we were equals.

Opposite: My mate Niall Quinn. Without the help, support and encouragement of my strike partner, I would never have scored so many goals for Sunderland.

Let the celebrations begin. Our dressing room after the Bury game was a scene of shouting, singing and plenty of champagne spraying!

Above: Allan Johnston became one of my closest friends at Sunderland. It's a shame things turned sour between him and the club.

Right: Lee Clark was a great player for us, but the boss was right to sell him.

Martin Scott and Michael Bridges: never regulars in our championship sides, but both made important contributions.

An Englishman's home is his castle, and here's mine taking shape in early 1999.

The 1997-98 First Division play-off final was a day of mixed emotions for me. It was great to score 35 goals in the season, but nothing could take away the pain of losing to Charlton.

Time for beach football. I didn't even know Sunderland was by the sea until I joined the club.

The icing on the cake to our championship win was my marriage to Julie in the summer of 1999.

I was delighted for Peter Reid when we won the Division One League Championship in 1998/99. A real player's manager and a very astute man. I owe him a lot.

Left: Winning the October Carling Player of the Month award in my inaugural season in the Premiership. I proved that I could flourish at the highest level by finishing 1999/2000 as the division's leading scorer. It was nice to be shortlisted for the Player of the Year award as well.

Right: I thought I played well leading the line for England against Belgium back in October 1999. I haven't had many chances in an England shirt, so you have to grab each opportunity as it comes.

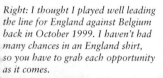

Left: Sunderland v Chelsea, December 1999 and I exact revenge for our opening day defeat at Stamford Bridge by contributing to a comprehensive 4-1 victory in the return game at the Stadium of Light. This was our best performance of the season.

The best partnership in Sunderland. My daughter Millie helps me get to grips with the First Division trophy.

coming out loud now thanks to our resident DJ, Danny Dichio.

As most people know, Deech was really into his DJ-ing during his days at QPR and was getting just as big a name in clubs as he was on the football pitch. But when he came to Sunderland, he made it clear that his days out late on the town were over. He now just spins his records as a hobby at home but always puts a few tapes together for the lads.

Trouble is, he's heavily into garage and house music and some of the stuff he plays sounds like the needle's stuck on the record. The older pros like Kevin Ball and Niall Quinn slaughter him for his music, but even they were up on their feet after the Swindon game.

The victory also set us up nicely for the second leg against Leicester. Wembley was just 90 minutes away for us, but we knew we had to be at our best to beat them on home soil. And I think that helped when it came to the game itself. We had nothing to lose and all the pressure was on Leicester, and the atmosphere in the dressing room was one of the most relaxed I had known. Of course, Bally and the gaffer were pumping us up, but there was plenty of banter and we were even talking about taking the game to penalties and letting Mickey take the last one! It was all light-hearted stuff but it took the heat out of the situation because in reality, this was one of Sunderland's biggest games of the past few years.

I just wish I had been a bit more focused before the game because I went on to have a stinker. It was another one of those matches where I just couldn't keep hold of the ball and didn't really look like scoring. Fortunately, the ten other players around me were pulling their weight and although Quinny scored, we drew the game 1–1. Unfortunately, it wasn't enough to get us to Wembley.

But it was in this game more than any other that we had caught the attention of the British football public. The tie was live on TV and not only did we match Leicester in their own backyard, we also outplayed them for long spells with some delightful football.

In the papers the following day, our performance had overshadowed Leicester's overall victory, and that was some consolation. But I would have loved to have played against Tottenham at Wembley. Obviously as an Arsenal fan, the game would have had extra meaning to me, and I know that my Dad would have loved it too.

He was a Spurs fan all of his life and although he tried to get me down to White Hart Lane, I wanted to watch Arsenal, probably because they were the more successful side when I was growing up, winning cups and league championships.

But as the years went on, supporting Arsenal had to be put to the back of my mind. As I was making my way as a YTS at Southampton, they were the only club I could think about back then. When I went into non-league with Baldock, I was playing every Saturday. I would never have the same passion for Arsenal as I did as a youngster but I still look out for their result after Watford's every Saturday.

To play at Highbury was still a big dream of mine, just like playing at Wembley, but that would have to stay in the back of my mind for now as we closed in on the championship.

Having beaten Bristol City and Wolves, we also took part in Sky's pay-per-view experiment against Oxford United. This meant kicking off at 6.00 pm at the Manor Ground and although it's great for the fans who can spend the afternoon down the pub and then watch the game, we were all really put out with the situation as it messed up our usual preparations for a Saturday afternoon match.

Having got up at our hotel at around 9.00 am, we then trained for a couple of hours, had our lunch and then went to bed in the afternoon, while the rest of the country were playing their games. It felt really strange and we just didn't feel our normal selves when it came to kick-off time.

The game finished 0–0 and whoever paid for the game must have wanted their money back. It was an awful afternoon all round and I bet Sky were none too pleased with the outcome, either. In hindsight, I don't think they could have picked a worse game that day. The only consolation for us was the fact that we'd got the Leicester game out of our system.

But I can't knock Sky too much. Their coverage of football is brilliant and the money they've ploughed into the game has certainly improved the standard in this country. I just wish that the powers-that-be would consider the players a little more. To kick off at 12 noon on Sundays and 6.00 pm is not ideal and I think the performances suffer because of it. But pay-per-view is likely to be the way forward for football in this country and, unfortunately, I can see strange kick-off times becoming more and more common.

Back-to-back home wins against Norwich and Portsmouth set us up nicely for our game of the season so far. The battle of the top two, Sunderland and Bradford at Valley Parade. If we could win this one, then we had a great chance of automatic promotion. But, in all honesty, I never thought the game would actually happen. All week long it had been raining heavily and having played at Bradford in the past, their surface is not the best in the world.

But we set out on our way and the rain continued to lash down. As we approached the outskirts of town, I looked out of the window and the place looked very familiar. Then I saw the Woolpack pub. 'Oi lads, we're at Emmerdale,' I shouted. But I wish I hadn't opened my mouth because I got slaughtered for owning up to being a big fan of the programme. Everyone else on the coach was expecting me to say 'EastEnders'!

The game itself could provide a good question for BBC's 'A Question of Sport' in a few years time. 'Who is the only Sunderland player to score a winning goal and keep a clean sheet in the same game?'

The answer: Niall Quinn. The game was a tight affair on a heavy pitch, I was having one of my better games and with half an hour to go Quinny's headed us into the lead. But then disaster struck. Thomas Sorensen was carried off injured and our chances of victory and, possibly, the championship, hung in the balance.

There was no reserve keeper on the bench, so who was going in goal? At 5ft 7in, I had no chance but then the calmest man on the pitch walked over to the bench and put the gloves on. It was Quinny, and he was superb, pulling off a couple of important saves. As we came off the pitch, Quinny was mobbed by the rest of us and it felt like we had almost won the league there and then.

Andy Marriott came in for the next game against Grimsby and it amazed me that he was still at the club at this point and hadn't asked for a transfer. Not only had he been stuck in the reserves all season, but the continual stick about his weight had reached new levels. All week in training he was getting derogatory comments about the size of his arse, which does actually happen to be the biggest in football. 'If he has to pick the ball out of the net, how's he going to get out?' etc, etc. Lee Clark's abuse of the poor boy was relentless and if I was in Andy's shoes, I would have left the club by now. But the big man has a great personality and he just lets all the stick go over his head. He went on to have a great game, keeping a clean sheet in a 2–0 win.

Thomas returned the following week in a game which we were all extra determined to win. Like the previous season against QPR, it was getting to a critical stage of the campaign and Bolton were the visitors. We knew that if we beat them, we'd be 15 points clear of them and well on our way to promotion.

Not only that, the gaffer had been reading in the Manchester press that Bolton boss Colin Todd was saying that his boys could still catch us up and that we would soon falter. The gaffer kept reading this every time he returned home to the north west and it had really got to him. He kept drumming Todd's words into us that week and by the time kick-off came around, we felt as if we owed them one. The lads were really wound up for the game, more than usual and there was only going to be one winner.

We cruised to a 3–1 win and I scored my 50th goal for the club but I was disappointed with Bolton, having tipped them at the start to come straight back up. Mind you, we were playing some unstoppable football now.

The bad weather was certainly taking its toll on the fixture programme and, not surprisingly, our next away game at Bury was postponed. So it was back on 'Soccer AM' for another stint in front of the Saturday morning cameras. I was on with Chris Bart-Williams and the bloke that used to play Alan in 'Coronation Street'. He's a Sunderland fan through and through and we had a good chat about the season in the bar after the show.

But the highlight for me was when I went out into the car park to play 'Chips', the game where you've got to chip the ball through the hole. I had travelled down to the show with my best mate Phil and behind the camera he was desperate to have a go, too. Now Phil's not a bad player but he blasted the ball almost over the Sky building and this was live on TV. Talk about an embarrassment. I was just praying that, as the best man at my wedding later on in the year, he wouldn't produce any similar clangers.

On the pitch, things just kept on getting better. From the Swindon game until the re-arranged fixture with Bury on 13 April, we would go on to win ten games and draw just two more. It was an incredible sequence of results and we felt invincible. And apart from Bradford, nobody else seemed capable of putting together a sequence of results to challenge us, which certainly made the task of winning promotion that much easier.

I was scoring regularly, so was Quinny, which was a good job because he had turned from hero at Bradford, to villain within the space of a few short weeks. A week before the Grand National, he gave a few of the lads a tip on a horse, which was a 'dead cert to win' according to our number nine. Now, as Quinny is horse mad and owns his own stables, a few of the lads were taking his advice and betting £100 at a time.

Unfortunately for those lads, the horse never even came out of the traps, let alone start the race and the following morning, they were absolutely fuming. 'Thick Paddy bastard' was one of the tamer expletives used to describe our legendary Irishman. Quinny, as usual, was last in and just walked through the door with a grin on his face and arms raised in resignation. 'Sorry,' he said and the expletives just became stronger and louder.

But to prove he does know his horses, the following week he told the lads to put their money on Billie Joe in the National itself. Naturally, all the boys declined and the horse went on to win, giving Quinny a nice little earner. He had come up smelling of roses and nobody could quite believe it. Talk about the luck of the Irish!

On the pitch our date with destiny had come. If we beat Bury, we would clinch promotion and be playing top-flight football next season. Nobody could catch us then, we would be safe.

But Gigg Lane is never an easy place to get a result and Bury have got some big, powerful lads in their side. Not only that, they were scrapping for their First Division lives.

And I was in big danger of missing the game altogether. This was the one game I was desperate to play in, but I was suffering from the effects of a throat virus. I was struggling to swallow and my mouth was full of ulcers, so the gaffer sent me home from training on the Monday.

Nothing, though, was going to stop me from playing the following night, so on the coach to the ground I was made to sit at the back on my own and when we got to the hotel, I was given a room on my own, just to make sure that I didn't pass my germs on to anyone else. I felt like a prisoner in my own football team.

But I was glad that I did play for when we walked out on to the pitch, it felt like another home game. Our fans had come in their thousands, filling three sides of the ground. Once we had seen them, we just knew we had to put on a show. And we made the start we had been looking for when I tucked away a penalty. By half-time, I had grabbed a hat-trick and we were 4–1 up. It was party time on the terraces and the fans were doing the conga. It was hard for the players because we wanted to join in too, but we still had 45 minutes of football to go. That's what the gaffer kept reminding us because the game was still not all over.

But we didn't take heed of his words and Bury came back into the game, scoring and then hitting the post. The gaffer was giving us a bit of an earful from the touchline until I scored my best goal of the night to seal the victory and with it, promotion. Having picked the ball up on the left, I cut in and steered the ball into the top corner of Dean Kieley's net. I felt elated but absolutely shattered and didn't even have the energy to run back to the half-way line. I just looked up to our fans and all of a sudden they're mobbing me. I was trying to tell them to get back so they wouldn't get arrested but they were having none of it.

Just before the referee was about to blow for full-time, he told us to make our way towards the tunnel, so that we could safely get back to the dressing room. I knew it was going to be like Swindon last season and that's exactly what happened. I managed to get back to safety, but I know the gaffer was besieged by the fans and almost had his tie ripped from his neck.

At Bury, there's a big corridor before you get to the changing room and I remember walking back down there thinking 'This is the best night of my life'. Sunderland had got promoted and I had scored four of the goals. It sounds a bit big-headed now but at the time, I thought I was the hero. I had won the game for Sunderland when, in truth, we had all played our part.

The champagne was flowing, there were socks being chucked about and everyone was singing and dancing. But for a moment, I just sat in the corner on my own unable to take it all in. To play in the Premiership was something that I had wanted to do all my life and now it was going to happen. There had been times when it looked as if I would never get the chance, but no-one could take it away from me now. I would at last have the chance to walk out at Highbury, play against Man United and touch the 'This Is Anfield' sign at Liverpool.

I wasn't thinking about the summer ahead or the fact that we had another four games to go before the season ended. I was already too busy putting pressure on myself by thinking that I've now got to score goals in the Premiership and that there would be no hiding place for me.

But I was determined to enjoy myself from that moment onwards. The dressing room celebrations were now at fever pitch and just as Mickey Gray's being interviewed by a woman from the BBC, she's hit by a dirty, sweaty jockstrap and the cheers go up even higher. It hit the poor girl right in the face and she didn't look too happy about it, so I'm sure she won't be coming to our dressing room again.

I was interviewed by Sky and I don't think anyone could make out what I said, such was the noise level and the inflatables which kept flying past the camera.

But we couldn't forget our loyal fans. We wanted to get back out to applaud them for their tremendous support all season, so as I walked back towards the pitch, I stopped off in the referee's room, picked up the match ball and went back out.

Even the Bury fans had stayed to applaud us and we were on the pitch for a good 20 minutes and to the supporters' credit, nobody ran on this time. I kept thinking what the pubs and clubs in Sunderland must have been like and the lads wanted to join them, so it was soon on the coach with the champagne as we headed back home.

We got back to our local pub in Durham shortly after midnight and the landlord kept the place open for us all night long. The whole squad turned up and we had a great night.

I got back home at about 4.30 am but I just couldn't sleep because the adrenalin was still pumping around my body.

I got up at about 7.00 am and put on a tape of the game which Sky had given me when I left the ground. I stayed up for the rest of the day, doing interviews down on the beach with *Shoot* magazine and Sky.

By all accounts the last of the drinkers left the pub at about 7.30 am and included in that bunch was Quinny. Apparently, Radio 5 Live phoned him up on air at 8.00 am for a quick interview and his wife answered the phone and said 'No chance, he's just got in!'

But the drinking had to stop because we had an equally important trip to Barnsley on the Friday night. A point would secure us the championship outright and we were deadly serious going into the game because we wanted to go up as champions.

Again, the kick-off was in some doubt as there was four inches of snow at Oakwell, but the groundsmen did well and the pitch was passed fit.

Looking back, I put in one of my best performances in a Sunderland shirt that night and the team played very well. Barnsley are no walkovers but we were unstoppable and cruised to a 3–1 victory. And just like at Bury, I scored late on and this was my favourite goal of the season, a curler from the edge of the box which their keeper Tony Bullock couldn't get anywhere near.

It was the best week of my life, with two games which probably made up Kevin Keegan's mind to select me for the England squad to face Hungary the following week. Again the celebrations continued but not quite on the same scale as the Bury game. Our bodies probably couldn't take the alcoholic punishment.

In fact, I went back home to Stevenage to be with my family and friends, who had their own little celebration planned for me, while the rest of the lads had a party planned in Durham.

Poor Allan Johnston was the talk of the party when I went in for training the following Monday. Now, as I've said, Johnno is a quiet, unassuming lad, who is almost teetotal. You can count the number of pints he's drunk on one hand but apparently he got into a right state that night.

He thought he was drinking pints of lager, which is bad enough for him, but little did he know that the lads were also spiking his beer with spirits and all kinds of shots. By the end of the night he was getting quite abusive and had to be carried out of the pub after he was found slumped asleep in the open urinal in the toilet. He was covered in urine and dead to the world. He has since admitted that he was up sick all night and had the worst hangover of his life. He also insists that he will never touch another drop of alcohol, and I don't think he's lying either.

From now until the end of the season it was party time. I was called into the England squad, along with Mickey Gray prior to our penultimate home game of the season against Sheffield United and life couldn't get better. The champagne was flowing, the phone never stopped ringing and the atmosphere at the club and in the city was brilliant.

But as I'd found out so many times, highs in football

are quickly followed by lows and I was about to suffer one of the most traumatic moments of my life.

We had now moved into our new house and my Mum had come up to stay for the weekend. After six months of building, everything was now complete and it was wonderful to finally have a place of our own again.

Mum had not been to see me play at the Stadium of Light since the opening game of the season against QPR. We had also invited up a couple of friends whom we had met on holiday the previous summer.

We got to the ground for the United game early, I sorted them all out with tickets and I was looking forward to keeping my goalscoring run going. As a team, we wanted to break the 100 point mark and there was no way we were going to let the season just fizzle out.

As usual, I got stripped and went out for the warm up. Then, at about 2.45 pm, the club doctor called me over to the edge of the pitch. I thought to myself 'What the hell does he want?'. At first I thought he just wanted to give me the results of a swab test I had taken prior to the Bury game when I had a throat infection. But it seemed a strange time to tell me that. It must have been more serious, and it was.

'Kevin, your daughter's been taken seriously ill, we've got to get her to hospital,' he said. In an instant, my whole world had collapsed. I immediately thought the worst. At that moment football and all the success meant absolutely nothing to me.

I quickly ran back down our tunnel and into the doctor's room and Millie was just lying there, lifeless. The doctor thought she had contracted meningitis and immediately gave her a penicillin jab, but I just thought that she was going to die. There had been a meningitis outbreak in the north east and Lee Clark's daughter had been rushed to hospital with the same symptoms earlier in the month. I was holding Millie with tears in my eyes and trying to comfort Julie, who was of course in a right state, at the same time.

There was absolutely no way that I could play football and the doctor went to tell the gaffer, who rushed in himself and told me to get to the hospital right away. We then sorted everything out with the referee and it was on to the Washington Hospital as quickly as possible.

As soon as we arrived, Millie was rushed into a cubicle for tests and a host of needles were stuck into her – it was heartbreaking to watch. Thankfully, after a couple of hours, she responded to the treatment and made a dramatic improvement. She was now out of danger.

It was a massive relief for us all and the specialist at the hospital reassured me that it was 99.9 percent certain that she would be okay. It was only when I heard his words that I joined up with the England squad on the Sunday night.

Two nights later she was released from hospital and it turned out that she had just picked up a viral infection, but it was the scariest moment of my life. I now appreciate Millie even more, having come so close to losing her and the whole episode hit home to me that there is much more to life than just playing football.

By the time I had returned home from Hungary, I was mentally exhausted. I don't think I'll ever have another couple of weeks like it: winning the championship, playing for England and seeing my daughter rushed to hospital with a serious illness.

In all truth, I'd had enough. I just wanted the season to end, there and then, so I could enjoy the summer break and come back re-charged and ready for the Premiership. But there were still two games to go, away at Stockport and then at home to Birmingham on the final day of the season.

Although I still felt okay physically, a trip to Edgeley Park was the last thing I needed, but I remember the gaffer saying to me, 'If you can play well and score today, after everything that's happened, then people will really start to sit up and take notice of you. You'll be the talk of the town.'

The game turned out to be a typical end of season affair, with both sides looking tired. But we still wanted to break the 100-point barrier and I think that extra determination was all that separated the sides.

I managed to score the only goal of the game, a shot from 20 yards which somehow managed to find its way into the net. The goal took our tally to 102 points for the season, equalling Swindon's total a few years back, so it was worthwhile playing in the end.

When I got home that Saturday night, I was absolutely shattered and crashed out as soon as I walked through the door. Our final game of the season was not until the following Sunday, so the gaffer gave us four days off, which at last gave me the chance to spend some time with Julie and Millie, who was now looking a picture of health again.

The Birmingham game would be the big finale, a

celebration of the season and the day when we would pick up the championship trophy and at last get our hands on our medals. It seemed a long, long time since we clinched promotion at Bury – so much had happened – but it was certainly worth the wait.

The club went to a lot of trouble to ensure that this would be a day that the fans and everyone connected with the club would remember for a very long time. There was a party atmosphere as I approached the ground – very similar to the Ajax game the previous season – while inside we had fireworks, a parachute display team and Republica playing live on the pitch. It was a hell of a day and I just wanted to get the game over so that we could get on with the celebrations.

Not that Birmingham were going to roll over for us. They were looking to cement their place in the play-offs and join us in the Premiership next season, and they looked really fired up. The game was not a classic by a long way and Birmingham inevitably took the lead, but we managed to dig deep into our reserves for one last time and we pulled the game around. I managed to score, which took me to 25 for the season, and it was great to do so in front of our own supporters.

Then it was party time as the trophy and medals were presented and at last we could call ourselves the champions. When we came back out on to the pitch for the presentation, the Queen classic 'We Are The Champions' was being sung by everyone. When it was the turn of me and Quinny to go up for our medals, there was a massive cheer which gave me goosebumps. It was incredible.

But the highlight for me was when the players were

allowed to bring their kids out on to the pitch for the celebrations. I got hold of Millie and had her in one arm and the championship trophy in the other, and it was wonderful. Despite all the people and the noise, she loved being carried around the stadium – she was a bit of a poseur, really. That's the one thing I'll always remember from the day and the fact that I knew that my Dad would have been looking down on us as proud as punch.

By the time we got back to the dressing room, I think that we'd all had enough of celebrating. We'd done all that at Bury and after the Barnsley game, and I think some of the lads were sick of the sight of champagne by now. The feeling inside the dressing room was one of relief, more than anything. Relief that we'd finally been crowned champions and relief that after the heartache of the previous season, we would finally be taking our rightful place back in the Premiership.

The victory wasn't just for the football club it was for the city of Sunderland, too. So the very next day we went on an open-top bus tour to show everyone the trophy. As we first got on to the bus, Bally – who has witnessed more than one open-top bus tour of the city – turned round to me and said, 'If you thought it was great yesterday, wait until you see this'.

And I wasn't to be disappointed. I just couldn't believe how many people loved the club until I got out into the streets and saw all the houses and shops decked in red and white and saw everyone so happy and proud at what their team had achieved. Everybody wanted to get a look as the bus went past and there were even people hanging from the roofs and trees.

We actually met up at the stadium a good hour-and-a-half before the procession, and there was food and drink laid on for the players and their families. The trouble was, the bar was free and when that happens, it's inevitable that you drink more than you usually would. Needless to say that quite a few pints were sunk before we had even got on the bus and within ten minutes of the journey, Lee Clark and myself were absolutely bursting to go to the toilet. We then turned around and realised that this was a bus, not a coach, and it had no toilets on board! We were in agony and getting bladder cramps; there was no way we could hold it in much longer.

There was only one thing for it. Downstairs, we had noticed a few litre bottles of mineral water, so we emptied them out of the bus windows, bent down on our knees and emptied our bladders. We were in stitches thinking that there were thousands of people outside in the street and there was us, down on our knees having a pee! I must have filled a bottle and a half, and when news got round of what we were doing, the rest of the squad followed suit. I plead guilty when I say that I felt so much better for it. I could now go back upstairs and join in the celebrations.

Then the bladder started to fill up again. What was I to do this time? The pains had come back as the beer had continued to flow but by this stage, we had run out of bottles. There was only one thing for it, back downstairs to use a big bucket which we had found. What a disgrace we were, and I can only apologise now to the wives and girlfriends who were on board at the time and any fan who had the misfortune of catching a glimpse of us 'in action'!

The best moment for me was when we turned the

corner to approach our final destination, the Seaburn Centre, and all you could see was a sea of red and white. It took my breath away and I made sure I took a few photographs.

To be honest, the whole procession dragged on a bit too long and by the time we had our civic reception and celebration dinner, we were all a little bit knackered. Not only that, we had a testimonial game to play the following night, for the former Sunderland player Jim McNab, so I didn't hang around too long into the evening.

The game was played at the Stadium of Light and it was the current first-team against an all-star Sunderland XI. We were allowed to play wherever we liked; I played at my old right-back position and really enjoyed it. The old boys beat us 4–2 which was hardly surprising because we had Deech at centre-half while Thomas Sorensen and Andy Marriott went up front. Those two slaughter us strikers in training when we fail to hit the target, but now they were getting a better idea of just how difficult it can be, and we were certainly getting our own back with a few choice words being shouted at them.

Quinny, naturally, took the No.1 jersey and it was a great evening all round. The crowd wasn't particularly big but I'm sure the ones that did turn up enjoyed themselves. They even got to see Marco Gabbiadini back in action for the club, and he showed what a class player he still is by scoring a hat-trick.

The celebrations finally came to an end that Wednesday night with the Red and White Ball, which was held at the stadium for all the players and staff of the club.

Everyone who turned up had to wear red and white and I was one of the more reserved on the night, wearing a black suit, white shirt and red tie. Bally went completely the other way with a circus outfit which, if we had all worn something similar, would have looked okay. But he really did stand out like a sore thumb. Quinny was going to put on his disco pants but bottled it at the last moment and instead opted for a red and white shirt which, of course, was the look for all fashion gurus like Quinny last summer.

We had a great night though, with a dinner and disco and there was also a fun room with a bucking bronco ride, casino and a running bungee jump, which the lads stayed well clear of, especially me after my injuries.

The best moment of the evening was when the chairman Bob Murray got up and put on a highlights film of the season, with Martine McCutcheon's 'Perfect Moment' playing in the background. It was really emotional looking back over the season, especially when we clinched promotion, and I must admit that I had a tear in my eye and a big lump in my throat.

But that was nothing compared to Bobby Saxton. When the video had stopped, the gaffer got up to thank us all for our tremendous season and then turned round and said 'None of this would have been possible without one man, Bobby Saxton'. With that, Bobby got up and gave him a big hug, before walking out of the room crying his eyes out. Although we've given him stick about it since, it was a really touching moment and showed the man's passion for the club.

Almost every club in the country finishes the season

with a relaxing break abroad and at Sunderland, we're no different. That week we headed off to Marbella for a four-day break. Although it was only a short break, we had been living in each other's pockets for the past couple of weeks, so it was long enough. And we still managed to have a good time.

We all like a laugh and a joke and nobody takes themselves too seriously but we also know when to get serious – the moment we step over that white line and on to the football pitch. That also reflects the manager's attitude to football. He doesn't mind us having a laugh and joke, but when it comes to the game, nothing else in the world matters for those 90 minutes. He demands that we give absolutely everything for the cause.

I don't think we could have paid him a greater compliment than winning the league. What we achieved was down to the gaffer. We carried out his instructions, played the way he wanted, and followed his style from the training ground on to pitch.

We shared his enthusiasm and determination and it proved to be a successful formula. A book is the ideal platform for me, on behalf of all the players, to thank him for our success. Without him, none of it would have been possible and I certainly wouldn't have been in the position I am today without his belief in my ability and decision to take a gamble on me when he could have opted for a much bigger name. Thanks, Peter.

Now it was time for me to put my feet up for the summer, recharge my batteries, and prepare for the new season, a season full of new challenges, new ambitions, new horizons.

CHAPTER NINE

England Calls

The weekend had passed. And having scored at Tranmere to bury our Prenton Park jinx, I was feeling good. I was in the middle of a hot streak in my first season at Sunderland, having scored eight goals in nine games, as we continued to pursue Middlesbrough and Nottingham Forest at the top of the First Division table.

On my way home from training that Wednesday, my mobile rings and it's Julie.

'You've been called up for the England 'B' squad.'

'Yeah, pull the other one. Anyway, how would you know?' I responded.

'Because the *Sunderland Echo* have just phoned up. They've been trying to get hold of you for your reaction.'

With that I put the phone down in disbelief. The blood was pumping, the body was shaking. Me? Playing for England? I still couldn't take it all in.

At this stage in my career, I hadn't given playing for my country a second thought and I didn't even know

England had a 'B' game coming up, that's how naive I was to the whole situation.

As soon as I got home, I phoned up Graeme Anderson at the *Echo* and he confirmed it. Then I put on the teletext and there it was in black and white. The England 'B' team to face Russia at Loftus Road on 21 April 1998 included K Phillips of Sunderland.

Of course, I looked for my name first but then I scrolled down the list and it included L Ferdinand, D Anderton and M Le Tissier to name but three. It was then that the penny finally dropped. I would be representing my country. It was the proudest moment of my career, although the nerves continued to make me shake.

Winning championships, making debuts and scoring goals is wonderful, but for a footballer there can be no greater honour than representing your country.

For me, I had dreamt of playing for England from the day I saw the 1982 World Cup in Spain on television. It was then that I realised the importance of playing for your country and that it is the pinnacle of any footballer's career.

Okay, this was not a full cap, it was a 'B' international, but it was certainly a step in the right direction. And let's not forget that I was still playing First Division football and had never represented my country at any level in the past.

Within minutes I was on the phone to my family and I was getting plenty of pats on the back in training the next day. It was brilliant for me to know that I had caught the attention of the England manager Glenn Hoddle.

Darren Holloway and Darren Williams had also been

called up and that certainly helped because I wouldn't have to go down to London on my own. I was far less nervous with them around.

Michael Holland drove us down to the Swallow Hotel in Waltham Abbey immediately after our home game with Crewe the following Saturday. We won the game 2–1 but I failed to get on the scoresheet, although that didn't dampen my enthusiasm. Unfortunately, Darren Holloway had to pull out of the squad after picking up an injury, so it was just the two of us who drove down with Michael for the game.

It was about 11.00 pm by the time we arrived at the hotel and we were met by one of England's PR women. She put the two of us in a room together but at this stage we hadn't met anyone else because the rest of the squad were already tucked up in their bedrooms.

The following morning, I was up nice and early – probably due to a lack of sleep – and the first player I bumped into was Le Tissier. It was the first time the pair of us had seen each other since I left The Dell and I wasn't sure that he'd remember me. But he came over and said 'You've come a long way for a right-back' and we had a good chat about the old days at Southampton. Having got on so well with Matt – one of the more senior pros in the squad – made me feel more at ease and I was then looking forward to training and the game itself.

I then walked into the hotel's reception and standing around were Trevor Sinclair, Rio Ferdinand, Frank Lampard, Les Ferdinand and Darren Anderton. It was all the London boys together and I can remember saying to myself, 'Christ, am I really good enough to be in the same squad as them?' After all, they were established Premiership players and just a few months earlier I was playing in the Second Division with Watford. But then I thought to myself, 'Of course I am. I've been playing well this season, scoring goals and would hopefully be playing against them before too long, anyway'. I had deserved my chance. I had to treat myself as an equal otherwise I wouldn't have been able to do myself justice when it came to the football.

We trained up the road at Enfield FC and on the coach on the way to the ground, I kept saying to myself 'Just don't mess up'. The last thing I wanted was for the rest of the squad to think 'what's he doing here?'.

We got stripped and ready for action and I was quite surprised at how light the training actually was. Peter Taylor and Dave Sexton took the coaching and most of the emphasis was on keeping possession and we had a couple of small-sided games.

We trained twice that Sunday, which is something I hadn't been used to before, and in the afternoon we did a bit more crossing and shooting, so that I could show the coaches exactly what I could do.

Les and Matt were fluffing a few shots and it was at that moment that I knew that they were only human and that I was doing just as well, if not better than them.

We did exactly the same on the Monday and it was while I was enjoying some shooting practice that I recognised someone standing behind the goal. It was my old Baldock boss Ian Allinson. He now works for a brewery and was delivering to Enfield's clubhouse. I went over to say hello. He was delighted with the progress I was now making but, unfortunately, I couldn't stand around for a chat and by the time I had finished training, he had gone. That was disappointing because I owe Ian a lot. He got me back into football and gave me the platform to show what I could really do, and as a striker, not a defender.

From the way training was going, I knew I was only going to be on the periphery of things when it came to the match that Tuesday night. On the morning of the game, Peter pulled me to one side and said that I would be on the bench but I was delighted with that. I never expected to play, so I wasn't too disappointed and he said that he would try to give me a run out towards the end of the game. I couldn't have asked for much more really and there was some consolation when Darren Williams told me that he had been picked, and I was delighted for him.

At this stage, I still felt that I was playing just another representative game, just like I had done when I was younger. It only really sank in that I was playing for England when our coach received a police escort from the hotel to the ground.

When you play for England, everything and everyone stops for you. And a journey which would usually take more than an hour, probably took about half that time. I felt like royalty as all the cars were halted for us as we drove through central London.

My first priority before the game was to get one of my shirts signed by the squad, and that now hangs proudly on my wall at home. I got changed in my usual way and I had no nerves at all at this stage, probably because I knew that I was only going to play a small part in the game.

When the match started, Ferdinand and Le Tissier, in particular, showed just how good they were. They oozed class from their very first touch of the ball and had an aura about them that no-one else on the pitch had.

The game itself was a one-sided affair and Matt was having the game of his life, scoring three wonderful goals as we cruised to a 4–1 victory. As the goals continued to fly in, I knew that I had a greater chance of a run-out and the moment finally came with 15 minutes left on the clock.

I came on for Les, shook his hand and took a quick glance up to the stand where my family was sitting. I knew that they would have been so proud of me and although Julie was watching the game back home in the north east, I knew she would have felt the same way.

My main priority was not to give the ball away and just keep everything simple. I did just that and nearly made a name for myself when I connected with a far post header that just sailed over the bar. If I had been a couple of inches taller, the ball would have been in the back of the net, but I wasn't complaining, I was just delighted to be out there.

In the dressing room after the game, everyone was buzzing and having played, I really felt a part of the squad now. I had been given a taste of international football and I wanted more. That's probably what the management wanted from me anyway, to get a feel for the England set-up and be hungry for it.

I was pleased with my contribution, however small,

and was delighted for Matt. I really thought he had done enough that night to win a place in Glenn Hoddle's World Cup squad. Unfortunately he would miss out and I really felt for him when the final squad was announced.

Michael Holland again picked us up straight after the game and I never even got a chance to have a chat with my family. We had an important game against Stoke that Saturday and we had to get straight back to the north east for training the following morning.

It was a sad moment when we had to say our goodbyes because with international football, you really don't know when you'll get another chance, especially when you're with Sunderland, playing in the First Division.

But when we got in the car, we were soon buzzing again and all we spoke about on the journey back was the game. I was just hoping that there would be a few more 'B' games arranged for the following season but with Euro 2000 qualifiers on the agenda after the World Cup, I wasn't holding my breath.

Instead, I channelled all my energies into doing well for Sunderland. Losing out on promotion was a hammerblow and by the time the new season came around, England was an afterthought, to be honest.

I was too old for the Under-21 squad and I knew that I would have to be playing in the Premiership to play for the full squad. That was, until Kevin Keegan was installed as manager.

It was purely coincidence that his appointment as England coach came at a time when I had got over my toe injury and was back at the peak of fitness and scoring goals on a regular basis. I had just scored five goals in two games to secure the First Division championship and I was the name in the headlines. Kevin had already gone on record as saying that if a player was doing well, he would give him a chance, and I couldn't have asked for much more than that. He had also said that he sees a lot of himself in me and that was a massive boost and a great honour to hear those words.

With England set to play Hungary in a friendly on 28 April, Kevin had an injury crisis in attack. Michael Owen, Les Ferdinand, Chris Sutton were all injured and when Robbie Fowler broke his nose, I thought that I might have a chance.

But Kevin had called up Chris Armstrong for the previous game with Poland, so I wasn't expecting to be picked. If I missed out, it was no skin off my nose because I knew that I really needed to be playing Premiership football to stand a chance.

Having wrapped up the league, Sky came up to do a feature on my rise to fame the following Wednesday. I met them after training and as I left the ground, there were rumours going around that I would be called up by England that lunchtime.

But I was still having none of it and continued on my way. For the first part of the interview, I took them to a local Dixons warehouse and then we went down to the beach to talk about my life at Sunderland. During the break between the two, at about 1.00 pm, I went back to my car to check my mobile phone and I could see that I had about seven messages left on it, which is more than I usually get in a week. But I didn't have time to answer them all then, and was just about to shut the door to continue the interview when the phone rang again.

'Phone Peter Reid straight away.' It was Julie and she thought I was in trouble. But from that moment on, I knew that I had been called up.

When I phoned the gaffer's office, our Youth Development Coach, Ian Branfoot, answered the phone.

'Congratulations Kevin, you deserve it.'

'Deserve what? I haven't heard anything,' I replied. And with that I think he felt a little embarrassed and handed the phone over to Peter, who had just walked into the office.

'Well done son, you've been picked for the Hungary game, along with Michael Gray,' he said.

'F*** off gaffer, you're joking, aren't you?'

In hindsight, maybe I shouldn't have said that, but I was still so shocked to hear his words.

We had a brief chat, I said my goodbyes and thanks and then got out of the car to carry on with the Sky interview. I was nervous, shaking and Sky caught it on film, which was brilliant to watch when I first saw it.

The guys from Sky said I looked as white as a ghost as we carried on the interview but I couldn't get the call-up out of my mind. I had just received the best phone call of my life and I just wanted to tell all my family and friends.

Not that I needed to because at 3.00 pm, the squad was announced to the public and my phone just didn't stop ringing from the moment I got home to the moment I went to bed, it was incredible.

But I still had the Sheffield United game and all the turmoil of Millie's illness to come before I could even start to think about England. But once she'd been given the all-clear on the Sunday, I flew down to London with Mickey from Teesside Airport that afternoon, still phoning home every couple of hours to make sure that everything was okay.

The England squad were staying at Sopwell House in Hertfordshire prior to the game, the hotel which is Arsenal's headquarters during the week. The two of us arrived early, two hours early in fact, and we spent the time looking around the hotel, which has a number of autographed shirts from national teams that have stayed there in the past. It then dawned on me that I would now be joining such illustrious company.

We were then given our room key and I decided to relax for a little while. I was expecting to share with Mickey, just like I had done with Darren Willliams on England 'B' duty. But I was surprised to be given a room all to myself. Then I thought 'Well, it is England' and I remembered that you only get the best if you are picked for your country.

Having freshened up and unpacked, the two of us came down to dinner and it was then that we bumped into a few more of the lads. Jamie Redknapp, Steve McManaman and Tim Sherwood were sitting there and they congratulated the pair of us. I was really nervous to be among the top boys but I knew Jamie from when we went to college together when he was at Bournemouth and me at Southampton, and he made me feel more at ease. Then I spoke to Frank Lampard and Rio Ferdinand, both of whom were on 'B' duty last season, and from then on I felt much more comfortable in my surroundings.

Nevertheless, me and Mickey were as quiet as hell around the meal table. You could tell we were the new boys and only spoke really when we were spoken to. At this point, we still hadn't met Kevin Keegan or Alan Shearer, who were both at the PFA Awards dinner in London, while the Man United boys had played Leeds that lunchtime, so would not be turning up until late.

So we then turned in, with a big day ahead of us and our first training session with the best players in the land.

As we came down for breakfast the following morning, everybody was there and although I was receiving plenty of congratulatory pats on the back for the call-up, most of the players had heard about Millie and were genuinely concerned about her health. Then I sat down with Kevin Keegan and he was great with both me and Mickey. 'You two deserve to be here, you can count yourself as one of the best in the country, so enjoy it,' he said.

He really put our minds at ease and his enthusiasm for football was really infectious. From the first moment we stepped out on to the training pitch, I could see that I would enjoy myself playing for him and he encountered a really positive reaction from the rest of the lads, too.

Just like my first training session with the 'B' squad, I felt a little nervous. I was now in the company of some players I had only ever seen on TV before, but I just kept remembering what Kevin had told me that morning. Although it was hard to take in, I was now an England player. I was one of the chosen few, and I had to keep believing that.

Training at Sunderland begins with a skills session where every player is put under the spotlight individually. The pressure really is on and if you mess up, you really get slaughtered. The lads were winding us up saying that the England boys start with the same routine and if we messed up there, we might as well pack up and come straight back home.

Mickey and me had a little laugh about it when we got changed ready for our first training session at London Colney, Arsenal's training ground. We got out on to the pitch, had a few stretches and prepared for our first training drill of the morning. 'Right lads, we'll start with a few ball skills,' said our coach Derek Fazackerley. What?! The two of us looked at each other in amazement. The lads at Sunderland were only joking but what they said had come true. It was skills time and the heart started to pump.

Thankfully the pair of us came through unscathed and the reason why both England and Sunderland have pretty much the same training routine is because Derek and our coach Bobby Saxton were together at Blackburn a few years back. That helped us, to be honest, because we knew what was to come before most of the other lads.

The training that morning was light-hearted as the United lads had only played the day before. But having missed out on Saturday's game with Sheffield United, I wanted to put in a bit more work and once everyone else had gone in to get changed, Kevin himself took me out for some extra training.

He's a great believer in quick feet and working with the ball, so that's what we did: plenty of skill work, strides and running with the ball. Then he would throw the ball up in the air and I had to return it with either one or two touches. It was intensive stuff but loosened me up a lot and I got more out of that than if I'd just gone out on my own for a run.

Kevin was constantly talking to me, constantly encouraging and on the way back inside he said to me, 'I've been really impressed with you, Kevin. You're going to start the game. Now I know that you are going to be nervous but just enjoy it and just do what you've been doing all season.'

I wasn't really listening at this stage, I was just in a dream world. *'I'm going to be playing, I'm going to be playing for England!'* I kept saying to myself. Kevin told me to keep it to myself for now and only tell the family, but I wanted to tell the world!

I must admit that when we got back to our hotel I did tell Mickey Gray because I was so desperate to tell someone and he was delighted for me. And I was pleased Kevin told me nice and early because it gave me plenty of time to get my mind right for the game.

We flew out to Budapest that afternoon and a few of the lads were concerned about our safety due to the on-going Kosovo crisis in the nearby Balkans. But as soon as we got on the plane, the chief of security told us that there were absolutely no worries and that soon put all our minds to rest. The war in Kosovo really put the football into perspective for us and that's why we all donated our match fees to the crisis. It was the least we could do.

My mind was totally on the football because I knew that I would be playing. It was hard not to tell anyone else but Kevin was good enough to tell me, so to keep quiet like he said, was the least I could do.

Once we'd stepped off the plane, it was another police escort through the city to our hotel. We trained the following morning and that was when Kevin announced the side. I would be partnering Alan Shearer, who came up to me and said, 'Kevin, you can come up and clean my boots afterwards'. But I just turned round to him jokingly and said 'Al, I'm in a position now where I can just tell you to fuck off!'

'You might as well, everyone else does!' he responded. And that broke the ice between us. Prior to this get together, I hadn't spoken to Alan at all since our Southampton days, but now we would be partners against Hungary the following night. It was an incredible scenario, and one Alan could barely get his head round, either.

'Al, if eight years ago when I was cleaning your boots, I'd have said that one day we would be partners for England, what would you have said?' I asked.

'I would have laughed right in your face,' was his response.

And I'm sure that's what everyone else at Southampton would have said, too. It was then that I had a little smile to myself, wondering what all my old coaches down at The Dell must have been thinking when they heard that I would be playing. Then I thought of Chris Nicholl and that day when I said I'd prove him wrong. Well, I couldn't do much more than play for England.

That afternoon, a press conference was held and I had

an idea that it would be a big one because we had to go to a different hotel for it. I was one of three nominated players to speak, along with Alan and David Seaman and we jumped in a car together to meet the awaiting media. I sat at the front and I was still thinking 'Christ, look who's in the back of the car with me'. But then I remembered Kevin's words and I had to keep saying to myself that I was now one of them, I was an England player.

And I realised just what that meant when I went inside, sat down at the table, looked up and was blitzed by hundreds of flashing cameras, microphones, dictaphones and notepads. It took my breath away. There must have been at least 40 journalists wanting to speak to me and my heart was pumping. I was a little nervous but was briefed by the England press people on what would happen and that I could stop whenever I wanted to. But once I'd got started, I really enjoyed it. I was creating so much interest due to my unconventional route to the top and I could sense that the journalists were really interested in what I had to say.

The feedback I got afterwards was that I handled myself really well and even Brian Woolnough from the *Sun*, who is supposed to be a hard person to impress, praised me for the way I had conducted myself.

I did a television piece for Sky, then a few radio interviews before it was time for the obligatory photocall for the national papers. We walked over to a nearby bridge, which had a statue of a lion in front of it. I'd seen the England players doing this before and now it was my turn. I tried to make it light-hearted and that's why I clenched my fists and pulled a bit of a face. I wanted to show them that although Kevin Phillips is deadly serious about his football, he likes a laugh too. You can't take yourself too seriously all the time and I think that came across when it was splashed across the papers the following morning.

What I did object to, however, was the fact that the *Sun* had tracked down Julie and Millie back home in the north east, and started taking pictures of them. Nobody asked for my consent and I knew nothing of it until I saw the paper the following day. I thought it was scandalous and although the two of them enjoyed all the attention, I saw it as an invasion of my privacy. I wonder how many of those journalists would like to see their family splashed all over the back pages?

Once I'd got back to the hotel, all I wanted to do was play the game and match day couldn't come quick enough for me. The preparation was very similar to what I'd been used to at Sunderland. Tactics stayed on the training ground and we'd gone through a few moves and set-pieces in training the previous day. So once we'd got up and had breakfast, we relaxed around the hotel until lunch time, had a sleep and left for the stadium later in the afternoon.

The preparation in the dressing room was the same, too. We had the ghettoblaster in the corner, pumping out some dance music but instead of Deech in control, we had an entertainment's man, who sorts out all the music and the videos for the hotel and the team coach. Again, the music wasn't the best, but there's no way I was going to slaughter this man like I do Deech. I would need a few more trips with England to do that!

Our dressing room was similar to what you get in American Football. We had individual lockers and a big drinks machine in the corner. And once I saw my England kit, not a replica that I'd worn when I was younger, but *the* kit, I started to get nervous.

I got changed and it was then time for the warm-up. Although the ground was not as big as the Stadium of Light, it was dark and the terraces just seemed to go right back into the haze of the floodlights. The pitch was just as I expected it to be: long, lush and quite sticky because it was a humid night.

In the warm-up, nobody really gave me advice, I was left to my own devices but in training Kevin told me just to stick close to Alan, whom I had a little chat with before we went back inside.

'I'll just work around you Al, you're the target man.'

'That's fine,' he replied. 'If I go into the channel, make sure you stay and when you go, I'll hold back.'

It was nothing complicated, just the usual way two centre-forwards work in every game of football.

Once we'd got changed and the referee's buzzer had sounded, it was now time for action. Everybody was shaking each other's hands and Kevin gave us one last pep talk.

'Just go out there, express yourself and most of all, enjoy it. Believe in yourself, you're all good players and just remember who you are.'

When I walked out of that tunnel on to the pitch, it was the proudest moment of my life and I doubt I'll ever feel as good as I did at that moment. I looked up to the sky to my Dad and then I lined up for the National Anthem. I didn't sing because I was so focused on the game and when I saw the TV highlights at home, the camera didn't even make it to me down the line, which was disappointing. But what they would have seen was a face full of concentration and a face determined to do well.

As the first-half wore on, I was playing well and enjoying myself. I could even have scored when Alan slid a ball through to me on the right-hand side of the box, but as I tried to shoot across the goal, I put the ball straight at the keeper.

That was the only moment of the entire trip that I look back on with regret. I should have put the ball in the net but when Alan put me through, I was conscious that I was playing for England and thought to myself 'If I score this, on my debut, I'm going to be a hero. This goal is going to be on a par with Michael Owen's against Argentina in the World Cup. The whole country's watching me and my name will be up in lights'. I thought all this in the split second I had, whereas when I'm with Sunderland, I don't think about anything except putting the ball in to the back of the net. If I'd been at the Stadium of Light, I would have scored, no question about it.

But on this occasion, it just wasn't to be.

The game itself was no classic and it petered out to a 1–1 draw. But I was pleased with my overall display, until my substitution late in the second half. I didn't try to do anything out of the ordinary. I kept things simple and, on reflection, I don't think I looked out of place at all.

I walked off of the pitch with my head held high, having handled the game, the press and the pressures well, which will hopefully stand me in good stead for the future. And as I put my tracksuit top on, Kevin came over and gave me a hug.

'Brilliant,' said the England boss, 'you've played really well.'

He didn't say much else until we got back to the dressing room, but then he went round to all the players to thank them for their efforts.

'Considering the circumstances, that was a great debut, I'm really pleased for you', he said to me. 'You're a full international now, always remember that. No-one can take that away from you.'

He was just as complimentary to Mickey Gray, who came on in the second half and put in some really testing crosses. He did his international chances no harm at all, and with the country lacking talented left-sided players, I expected him to remain very much a part of Keegan's plans.

And that was it. It was time to head back home and prepare for our trip to glamorous Stockport. The phone continued to ring, especially from the local press for the rest of the week, all wanted to know how I enjoyed the game. I ended nearly every call with the same answer. 'It was a wonderful experience, but I don't expect to be included for the big qualifiers against Sweden and Bulgaria.'

That's what I honestly thought and when the

Sunderland boys left for Marbella for our break at the end of May, I thought that was the start of my summer. However, when I got back, there was a letter waiting for me, written on official FA paper, stating that I was in the provisional squad of 30 players for both games. I was delighted and honoured, especially with two such crucial games to be played. Mickey, too was included and although I was due to take the family away before my wedding in June, I was happy to sacrifice it for Wembley.

Now all I had to make sure was that I didn't get injured playing against Liverpool at the Stadium of Light that night. The game was to celebrate 100 years of the Football League, the holders of the Division One trophy against the team which has won it the most times.

'Haven't we had enough bloody football for one season?' I said to the gaffer in the lead up to the game. 'We should be resting now ready for next season or for international games should anyone be selected.'

In all honesty, he agreed but his hands were tied to a certain degree because it was a prestigious game and both teams had already agreed to field full strength sides.

So I took to the field and after the break scored a good goal with a diving header, and at that point I was just pleased to sign the season off on a winning note. But a few minutes later, I went to chase the ball on the far side of the pitch with Phil Babb when all of a sudden I felt something go in the back of my leg.

I was on the ground writhing in agony. My hamstring had gone and my season had abruptly ended. I was in tears as I was stretchered off the pitch and all I could think about was missing out on the England games. Then anger took over and all I kept saying was 'Why did I have to play in this poxy, meaningless game?'

As the gaffer already knew what my feelings were towards the game, he was devastated for me. He also knew exactly what the England call meant to me. So instead of going home and getting myself geared up for another international call, I spent the night in the Washington Hospital to find out the extent of the damage.

It turned out that I had a 2 cm tear in my right hamstring and I would not play again that summer. I would be fit in time for pre-season training but that was small consolation to me at the time. I wanted to play for England, nothing else mattered, and now I hope that the club will think twice in future before making us play in such games.

I'd had enough. I'd come back down to earth with a bump and was going out of my way to avoid the phone at all costs. I didn't want to speak about the injury, it was too painful in every respect. A couple of evenings after the game, the phone rang.

'If it's for me, I'm not in,' I said to Julie, as I sat down to watch my old mates Watford in their play-off semi-final at Birmingham.

'Er, I think you'd better Kev, it's Kevin Keegan.' And with that I was on the phone in a flash, forgetting all about my injury hell.

He had called up to see how I was and he then told me that I would have definitely made his final 22 with a view to playing some part in both games. I was absolutely gutted when I heard that, but the pain was eased by the fact that he had bothered to phone me up to see how I was.

'I know it's only a small consolation, but I'd like you still to come down to be a part of the squad, get treatment from our physios and walk out at Wembley for the Sweden game,' he added. 'Do you fancy that?'

I didn't even need to answer, I thought it was a superb gesture and it just proved again what a brilliant man-manager he is. Every footballer you meet has the utmost respect for Kevin Keegan and I now know why.

The nerves were back again, even though I wasn't even playing. Julie drove me down to the hotel at Burnham Beeches and my heart was pounding as I knew that this time there were a few more big guns in the side, the likes of David Beckham, Sol Campbell and Andy Cole.

It was 6.00 pm in the evening and once again I was early. The rest of the squad would not be turning up for another hour yet, but I met our physios Gary Lewin and Alan Smith in reception and they soon made me feel welcome. So welcome, in fact, that within minutes I was already up on the couch having treatment on my hamstring.

It would be the first of three daily treatments I would have: one in the morning, then at 6.30 pm and another just before I turned in at 9.30 pm. 'If I'm not fully fit when I come away from here, I'll never be,' I said to them.

It was then time to go down for dinner and meet the rest of the lads. I hadn't travelled with Mickey this time and I banged on his door at about 6.50 pm to go down with him. Again the lads congratulated us and Kevin Keegan made me feel so welcome again but in a way, I didn't feel like I belonged. I knew I wasn't in the squad, and although I was honoured to be asked along, I felt on the fringe of things for much of the time.

That was highlighted the following morning when we all went to Bisham Abbey for training. As we walked past reception, there were a couple of England shirts for the lads to sign. My signature wasn't required and that was disappointing.

It was the same out on the training ground. While the lads were being put through their paces, I was having treatment before spending some time in the gym for some circuit training, upper body weights and some stretches. By the time I went out to watch the lads in action, they'd worked on tactics and were now just having a mess about five-a-side game.

I really envied them. They knew they had a goal to aim for at the end of the week and would find themselves in different training situations each day. Nothing could be further from the truth for me. I had the same treatment regime each day and frustration was starting to lead to boredom. If only I hadn't played that bloody Liverpool game.

At least we were given Monday afternoon off. We had the option of going shopping in London, playing golf or a trip to the cinema. I would have loved to get in 18 holes but because of the injury, I opted for the latter.

The highlight for me was on Thursday when we got to train at Wembley. I was now feeling much better and while the lads were put through their paces, I did some jogging and some light ball work.

It was great to be back and even Mickey had a smile on his face as we walked out on to the immaculate surface. Although Wembley has a capacity of 80,000 it doesn't look half as big when it's empty, although there is still a tremendous aura about the place. Once I'd got a feel again for Wembley, I now had a feel for the rest of the week and I was looking forward to the game. For Mickey, he was even more enthusiastic than me, knowing that he could actually play.

And the play-off final game came back to us again. On the day of the game, there were many comparisons: the route to the stadium, the crowds, the dressing room and the atmosphere out on the pitch.

But this time I felt like royalty. Again, we received a police escort to the stadium and everything and everyone stopped for us. People trying to hit deadlines and trying to earn a living stopped for us in an instant. It really was a day of mixed emotions and although I walked out with the team and around the gravel track, I never sat on the bench but up in the stand with Gareth Southgate and Emile Heskey. There were a few shouts of 'Super Kev' as I walked past, which gave me a lift, and I noticed quite a few Sunderland fans who had come down to give Mickey plenty of support.

The game itself was a major disappointment for the fans and players alike. The fact that Paul Scholes got sent off disrupted our play and limited our attacking options. I also felt sorry at this point for Mickey because he had got forward and delivered a couple of great crosses up until this point but then had to concentrate more on his defensive responsibilities.

The final whistle was greeted with a chorus of boos but I felt for the players out there. Let's not forget that we had ten men, let's not forget that we were playing a very good side in Sweden, and let's not forget that some of our players had played 40 or 50 games that season. I think David Beckham had played close on 60 matches, with Man United's European and FA Cup runs, and that means tremendous wear and tear on the body.

It really is time something should be done. We play far too many games in this country and it's clearly having a detrimental effect on our national team. Maybe it's time for the League Cup to be scrapped; and we should definitely consider a mid-season break. Oh, and let's make sure we end these meaningless friendlies at the end of the season. Especially the ones against Liverpool. At the Stadium of Light!

The fatigue factor was even more evident during the draw against Bulgaria the following Wednesday. By now I had left the squad and was in Cyprus, but managed to catch the second half and the game looked like it was being played at half pace. It was a poor match all round, but I felt confident we could still pull results out of the bag in our last two qualifiers against Poland and Luxembourg.

Personally, the two results filled me with mixed feelings. If world-class players like Alan Shearer, Robbie Fowler and Andy Cole were struggling to make an impact, then what chance would have I stood? But then again, none of the forwards on show made a real impact, which I hoped would leave the door open for me.

But two caps and an end of season call up was more than I ever could have dreamed of. I'd had a taste of international football now, I liked it, and there could not be a greater incentive now for me to go on and produce a successful season for Sunderland in the Premiership. If I could repeat my past glories in a Sunderland shirt in the top-flight, then I knew I would have further opportunities to slip on that famous white jersey with the three lions on it.

CHAPTER TEN

Premiership New Boys

I felt a degree of apprehension as the opening-day fixture with Chelsea loomed ever closer. The lack of activity in the transfer market was causing not only me, but a few of the other lads, concern. Our two major summer signings remained Steve Bould and Stefan Schwarz and although both are deeply respected and experienced figures, I felt they were players coming towards the end of their careers. In my opinion, we needed players at the zenith of their game, who would be able to take Sunderland forward for the next four or five years.

My anxieties were heightened following our final warm-up game against Rangers at Ibrox. Although the Glasgow giants had proved invincible in their domestic championship, we felt there was a chasm between them and the top Premiership sides. A solid performance would put us in good stead for the game at Stamford Bridge, a defeat would only fuel further the scepticism.

We endured a torrid evening and walked off the pitch

resoundly beaten. Rangers had put on a show in front of their devoted masses, while we were the vanquished no-hopers. We had been outplayed in every department and seemed to be affected by the lack of balance in the side, caused primarily by the absence of Allan Johnston.

Our new Danish recruit Carsten Fredgaard came in to fill the void on the left, but it was inevitable that he would struggle to adapt to his new surroundings. I trudged off the pitch under no illusions that this would be a season of sweat and toil if we were to retain our top-flight status.

I was bemused and disappointed by the entire Allan Johnston affair. He was in no doubt that he wanted to see out his contract and leave for Rangers, a club he has supported since a lad. But having shared a room with him and knowing his burning desire to do well, I was disappointed he would not commit himself and test himself in the most exciting, if not the best, league in the world. He would have benefited greatly from the experience, likewise Sunderland, who found the left-hand outlet a problem area for much of the season.

But once Johnno had made his intentions clear, he found himself banished to the footballing wilderness by Peter Reid. Loan spells at Bolton and Birmingham would follow a lean time in the reserves before he completed his switch to Ibrox in the summer of 2000. It was a sad end for a player whom I had grown close to, but I could understand the gaffer's stance. If you don't want to wear the red and white shirt, why should you be a part of the set up? Speaking to Allan, I know he found the situation hard to deal with at times in 1999/2000, but he left with my best wishes and I'm sure he'll be a major success in Scotland.

Carsten, too, would find himself banished to the reserves, having struggled to adapt to life in the Premiership. The step-up from Lyngby in the Danish League proved insurmountable and having been caught out of position for one of the goals on the opening day at Chelsea, he would rarely get another chance. But I've seen enough in training to suggest that he still has a future at the club. He has pace and a great left foot; now he needs the confidence to go with it.

The doubts and internal squabbling had to be put to the back of our minds for that trip to Stamford Bridge, arguably the toughest and most intimidating opening fixture imaginable to the 1999/2000 season. Chelsea had high hopes of winning the Premiership and lined up for the game at full strength. I remember warming up and catching a glimpse of players like Zola, Desailly, Deschamps, Leboeuf and Poyet. It was an impressive array of talent and a formidable barrier we would have to breach. It then sunk in – we were back in the big time and I had arrived in the Premiership.

We didn't start the game too badly but Chelsea soon found their stride and their class illuminated an already red-hot afternoon. We had no answer and having fallen two goals behind at half-time, we were kidding ourselves in the dressing room that we could get something out of the game.

We proceeded to lose by four goals and Desailly proved to be one man mountain I just could not climb. I found the pace at which Chelsea knocked the ball around to be much quicker than what I'd experienced in Division One and their players were far more comfortable and competent on the ball. The speed of thought was also something we would have to come to terms with. You do not have to be the quickest or strongest of players but if you possess a brain that is two or three steps ahead of your opponent, you will be an undoubted success at this level. That day, players like Zola and Deschamps were five or six steps ahead of us.

In hindsight, the lesson handed out was the best thing to happen to us. 'Welcome to the Premiership!' said the gaffer as we returned, downtrodden, back to the dressing room, having observed an exhibition in footballing perfection. There was only one direction we could now head in.

Respite came in the form of our promotion counterparts, Watford. The game would prove to be the perfect antidote to the Chelsea game and we soon recorded our first three points in front of a full house at the Stadium of Light. In all honesty, the quality of opposition was light years behind what we'd experienced at Stamford Bridge, but it still took us 45 minutes to get into our stride. I seem to have a habit of scoring against my former team-mates and having got off the mark with a penalty, I made the game safe with an emphatic strike from 25 yards. Some people might belittle the goal as it came against the eventual basement boys, but it meant the world to me. It was the goal that signalled my arrival in the Premiership and it gave me the springboard to launch a prolific season. The confidence was back both for myself and the team.

But a truer test of whether we'd learnt anything from the Chelsea debacle came in the form of Arsenal, who were the next visitors to the Stadium of Light. Another outfit packed with multi-national superstars, there was a danger of being over-run again, but the gaffer ensured we wouldn't suffer another humiliation.

To counter Arsenal's experience and technical superiority, he opted for a 4-5-1 formation, leaving yours truly as the loan striker. Not an ideal situation from a personal perspective, but it proved a point as we came away with a creditable 0-0 draw.

On reflection, Arsenal probably deserved the win, having hit the woodwork on a couple of occasions, but it was a fantastic point for us. I barely had an opening all game, although it was a wonderful moment to run out against the side I had supported since a child.

The 'safety first' policy adopted that day would continue for the trip to Leeds United. If I'm brutally honest, it was a situation I was far from happy with, nor did I want to get used to.

As the lone striker, you have to work tirelessly for the full 90 minutes and hope your midfielders will provide some welcome support. You have to be where the ball is and you have to make it stick. I had been so used to glancing balls into the channel for Niall, that it was a learning experience for me, but I had to remember that the team's welfare came before that of Kevin Phillips.

We applied ourselves much better at Elland Road but, having gone a goal up, our hard work was eradicated by an off-the-ball incident which at best can be described as gamesmanship, at worst, cheating by Lee Bowyer.

Alex Rae had run into the midfielder's path and for reasons only he can answer, Bowyer fell into a crumpled heap, writhing in agony. It was an innocuous clash but having already picked up a yellow card, Alex was given his marching orders as the crowd bayed for his blood. We proceeded to lose the game 2–1 but I felt that with eleven men on the pitch, we were playing well enough to win. The game left a bitter taste in the mouth and we remained without a win at Elland Road for almost 30 years.

I found myself embroiled in controversy that day, having earned a first-half penalty. I was accused by the Leeds players of diving, having gone tumbling under a challenge by Lucas Radebe, but I can honestly say that I have never dived for a penalty in my life. He pulled me back, it's as simple as that. If there is contact at this level, you have to go down – such are the high stakes in the game today – but my conscience is clear. The wall of venom that faced me was something I'd never experienced before, but I took the kick with typical aplomb and it was a sweet moment to hear the celebrations from our pocket of fans at the other end of the ground.

The vitriol I experienced that day was nothing compared with the Tyne and Wear derby game at St James' Park. In my opinion, this is the biggest derby game in the fixture calendar, far outweighing the Mersey, Manchester and north London equivalents. Those games might have the atmosphere and the passion but they certainly don't have the hostility and hatred that exists between our sets of supporters.

The build-up began prior to the Leeds game, which I found a little bemusing, but following that injustice, we were looking to let our frustrations out on our local rivals.

The preparation for the game was no different to any other but we were able to prepare in a low-key manner thanks to the ongoing dispute between Newcastle boss Ruud Gullit and his captain Alan Shearer, which was making back-page headlines both locally and nationally. The turmoil at St James' Park had been reflected in their appalling start to the season and the relationship between the feuding parties had reached fever pitch by the time we visited on 25 August. It was to our relief and amusement that Gullit had dropped both first-choice strikers, Shearer and Duncan Ferguson, for the game. We had been dealt a psychological shot to the arm.

The news filtered through on the afternoon of the game and from that moment on we were no longer the underdogs. Our defenders were particularly happy with Ferguson's absence, as the big man can be a real handful when he's on song. As we arrived at the stadium we were pumped up, but not hailing from the area helped as I could distance myself from the hype and was able to treat the match as just another game. Don't get me wrong, I desperately wanted to win for our fans, but I could maybe relax a little more than some of the local lads.

The conditions that night were nothing short of farcical. It had rained all day, but we were greeted by a torrential downpour which persisted for the full 90 minutes. It certainly put a dampener on the atmosphere, not helped by the sorry allocation of tickets give to our fans — just 300 were admitted, which was shocking for such a big game.

I can understand the safety considerations associated with such a hostile game, but surely there is enough policing and closed-circuit television monitoring to allay those fears? The police know who the known troublemakers are in the north east, so I couldn't see that being a major problem.

Thankfully, our loyal masses were able to watch a live broadcast of the game at the Stadium of Light, so we knew we had 20,000 fans watching us in spirit, if not presence.

To their credit, Newcastle had the better of the first-half exchanges and deserved their one-goal lead. Quinny came closest to opening our account when he was inches away from my low drive, but we had opened up their water-tight defence and that gave us heart for the second period, which was started with a clean, dry kit.

Playing towards our fans, we found another gear and there was an inevitability about Quinny's 64th minute equalizer. In all honesty, I thought Niall had missed because he didn't really get a clean head on the ball, but as it skimmed off the sopping surface, it beat Tommy Wright and sparked a wave of emotion from our band of supporters.

There would be only one winner now and we only had to wait another eleven minutes before the killer blow was struck. Having been put through by Gavin McCann, I somehow brushed off the close attentions of Nikos Dabizas and had only the advancing Wright to beat. Unfortunately I hit the ground, such was the saturation underfoot, and the ball was parried to the edge of the six-yard box. As I went to regain possession, I could sense Quinny closing in on goal but could also see defenders running goalwards, so I instinctively went for the chip. I knew Quinny had a chance of reaching the ball if I hit it too straight, but I've never hit a cleaner ball and to see it nestle in the back of the net was truly incredible. That goal rates as one of the pinnacle moments of my career; throughout the stadium it sparked a deafening silence but for the Mackems, who had broken the hush with unbridled joy.

The scenes at the final whistle are still so vivid. Having thanked our fans, we walked up the steps in the tunnel to the dressing rooms and that's when the screaming and shouting began. We drove back into town to pick up our cars and there was a carnival atmosphere with people dancing in the streets. The fact that they were drenched was irrelevant – they were ecstatic that we had put one over our biggest rivals, and so was I.

Such is the fanaticism in the north-east for football, I felt almost suffocated whenever I stepped out in town following the result. People wanted to talk to me, congratulate me, even be abusive (Magpie fans, obviously), but it is not in my nature to lock myself away, despite these newly-acquired trappings of fame.

I can almost feel the burning sensation of the stares, but I'll still visit the local supermarket, use local amenities and have holidays which might not be considered the 'vogue' among footballers. Indeed, this summer I took the family to Tenerife for a short break following Euro 2000 and fellow holidaymakers were puzzled that I hadn't headed elsewhere. But why should I change? I'm still a working class lad at heart and I'll always stay true to those roots. Of course, it's nice to be able to buy the finer things in life, but I never lose sight of where I came from.

Our unrelenting induction to Premiership life at last started to ease. We knew that seven points from the opening five games would provide a base on which to build as we prepared for Leicester, Derby, Sheffield Wednesday and Bradford – teams who we knew would either figure in mid-table or a relegation battle. We could now look forward to putting a run together in our bid for Premiership survival.

Having seen me score in the Sky televised game against Coventry, Kevin Keegan stuck to his summer promise and brought me back into the England squad for the Euro 2000 qualifiers against Luxembourg and Poland. Despite my rich vein of form, it was disappointing not to figure in either game, particularly the 6–0 defeat of the part-timers, which had turned into an exhibition match by half-time. I came away downcast, but not disenchanted as I knew that if I kept scoring goals, my chance would surely come. I still had to establish myself at the highest level and, with two play-off games against Scotland now added to the agenda, time was still on my side.

Sunderland's four straight Premiership wins that followed the internationals far exceeded our expectations, but we just grew in confidence with every passing game. Both on and off pitch, there was a togetherness, almost a feeling of invincibility. The personal highlight for me was the hat-trick I scored at Derby, a memorable moment in my fledgling top-flight career. Of the three, the second goal is my favourite as I adjusted my body and volleyed the ball across the face of the goal before it nestled in off the post. Nick Summerbee was in a far better position to shoot, so I had to make sure it went in to save myself from the wrath of 'Buzzer'!

We also witnessed the emergence of young Gavin McCann during this period of the season. Kevin Ball still remained an integral part of the squad, but you could sense the gaffer veering towards young Gavin more and more. He was particularly impressive in the Leicester game and was quickly making the transition from reserve-team player to Premiership star. Strength, skill, agility, he has the armoury to become the ultimate central midfielder and a future England international. But for his cruciate ligament injury, he would surely have run me close for the club Player of the Year trophy and his Young Player award speaks volumes for the impact he made.

Bally was eventually sold to Fulham to team up with Paul Bracewell, Andy Melville and Lee Clark, although I thought his departure was somewhat premature. Every team needs a player of his calibre and I thought he might have played more. One way or another, Gavin would not last the excesses of an entire Premiership season and Bally would have been the ideal replacement. The gaffer, however, did not see it that way and he has since been proved justified in his decision.

My reservations regarding the signing of Bould and Schwarz had also proved unfounded. Both had settled tremendously well and Bould was looking invincible in defence, the colossus he had become famed for at Arsenal. He gave the back four stability and confidence and it was no coincidence that our dip in form would come at a time when he was out of the side with a toe injury. Another player who could so easily have pipped me for the club Player of the Year accolade, had injury not curtailed his season.

Schwarz was signed as our inspirational central midfield lynchpin, but circumstances dictated a left-sided position instead. He provided the balance which we had lacked in the early games and although not an out-and-out winger, he was a strong creative force for the team. Again, injury would prove his downfall and he fell under the curse of the achilles tendon injury which seems to be prevalent in football at the moment. I felt great sympathy for Stefan, who also missed Euro 2000, a tournament I know he wanted to use to bring the curtain down on his Sweden career.

Nine goals in ten games provided me with the confidence to break my international duck against Belgium, a game which would be played at the Stadium of Light. It was a bold decision by the FA to switch the game away from Wembley, but I don't think they could have chosen a better, more passionate venue. Naturally I was delighted and excited to finally start another international, but I don't think Kevin Keegan had any other option.

In hindsight, I wish the game had been played at Wembley because the pressure on me was suffocating. I couldn't really relax, prior to the game or throughout its duration, and my performance was, naturally, affected.

My partnership with Alan Shearer just didn't click and I was struggling with the tight man-marking that is common-place in international football. To remain an integral part of Keegan's plans, it was vital that I linked well with Alan, but it just didn't happen for us on this occasion.

I created two chances, for Steve Guppy and Frank Lampard, but carved out very little for myself and there was an air of inevitability when I departed from the game after 58 minutes. Kevin took me aside later and said I had a bad game and could work a lot harder. I agreed with him, but I felt that I deserved longer on the pitch to demonstrate my true ability.

That has been typical of my international career to date. I feel as if I'm never going to get a full 90 minutes which irritates me because it's in the latter stages of games that defenders tire and you inevitably get more chances in front of goal. When you know you're likely to be hauled off, you just cannot relax, and tend to snatch at opportunities as if in a race against time.

I would rather forget my performance against Belgium, which is a pity considering it was played in front of my own fans. It certainly cost me my chance of playing some part in the Scotland play-off games; however, I could have scored a hat-trick against Belgium and still found myself on the bench, now that Michael Owen was free from his hamstring problems.

I was not in the best frame of mind following the international and thankfully Peter Reid rested me for the midweek encounter at Wimbledon in the Worthington Cup. We lost the game in extra-time but I was already focused on our forthcoming Sky game with Aston Villa, when I could show the nation what I was really about.

Another two goals put paid to any lingering

reservations the pundits might have had about my ability to score at the highest level. Indeed, the likes of Ian Rush, Gary Lineker and Ian Wright were now singing my praises. I was being held in a similar esteem to these great names and had emerged as the latest natural goalscorer to make a mark on the Premiership.

People ask me whether I had to change my style following the step up from the Nationwide League, but I can honestly say that it all came naturally. Of course, you have to work harder and I practise more because chances are less frequent, so I'll spend time after training just hitting the target: inside the box, outside and from the penalty spot. Your brain needs to be sharp, but in terms of scoring goals and getting into the right positions, it was just happening spontaneously.

If I could explain how it happens, we'd all be able to score goals, but it's just a natural reaction – as if the ball is a magnet to me.

As a team, we had fast emerged as the surprise package of the season. Mid-table obscurity was our predicted battleground but here we were, almost a third of the way through the season, and on course for a place in Europe. The expectation levels were growing and even the players were believing in the hype, but I was still worried that injuries and suspensions would ultimately prove to be our downfall.

And we were certainly not helping ourselves in the disciplinary department. Steve Bould lost his head at West Ham and was rightly dismissed, while at Boro, Chris Makin suffered a similar fate. Both games were drawn affairs, when victories were certainly in our grasp and, following Alex Rae's earlier red card at Leeds, the situation was causing concern for the gaffer.

Alex would also receive his marching orders on the final day of the season at Tottenham and find himself embroiled in controversy following an elbowing incident with Derby's Darryl Powell in the home draw at the Stadium of Light. The Rams midfielder had blood pouring from a cut and once the final whistle had gone, he raced towards Alex in the tunnel. Thankfully, further confrontation was avoided but Alex was disciplined by the club for his actions.

Alex is such a mellow character off the pitch, but, like a lot of players, he so badly wants to win that his passion boils over and he sometimes does things he regrets. He's always been a fiery character, even as a youngster at Millwall, but I don't care what you say or do to him, you can't change him and I don't think he'd be the same player if you tried. When he's on song, Alex is a tremendous asset to our side.

Our disciplinary record possibly reflects the manager's passion for the game but there was no doubt the situation was costing us points. You undeniably need fire in your belly to be a success – just look at Manchester United, Leeds and Arsenal – but they have the squads to cope with absentees. At this moment in time, we cannot afford to tread such a fine line.

My scepticism about my place in the England side would ring true as I found myself confined to the subs' bench for the first leg play-off game at Hampden Park. It was a great experience to be involved in a fixture which might never happen again, and the hostility in the crowd was similar to that I experienced at Newcastle. To again emerge on the winning side was fantastic.

But it was, nevertheless, a difficult day for me. As a substitute, you warm-up as if you're ready to play, but then sit on the bench and get cold again. You have to remain focused on the game, knowing that you could be called on at any point, but when Andy Cole replaced Michael Owen, it was hard for me to stay motivated. But I remained positive, knowing that millions of people would have given their right arm to be where I was, including myself just five years earlier.

Two well taken goals by Paul Scholes set us up nicely for the return leg at Wembley on the Wednesday night and although there was great elation in the dressing room, it was fairly low-key. It was still only half-time in the tie, and I was hoping to make my mark at the Twin Towers.

Having spent a couple of days with my family, I returned to Burnham Beeches only to be told that I hadn't even made the bench. I felt gutted; it was a bitter pill to swallow and I wanted to know what I'd done wrong. But it's not in my character to seek a confrontation with the manager, so I just kept my head down and vowed to keep scoring goals for Sunderland. It rankled with me that I still hadn't played at Wembley for my country and time was running out, with the old stadium soon set to be demolished.

The general consensus was that Michael Owen and myself were too similar and that Keegan saw the Liverpool lad as Shearer's first-choice partner. The comparisons continued the following weekend when Liverpool were the visitors to the Stadium of Light, with the game billed as a 'Phillips versus Owen' showdown. He certainly showed his pace to score a good goal as Liverpool returned to Merseyside with a 2–0 win. They had inflicted on us our first home defeat in 12 months but I felt it could have been so different if I'd connected with a simple header from just six yards. I still have no idea how I missed the chance, maybe I was just too relaxed, maybe that was the case for all of us.

So it was first blood to Owen, according to the papers the following morning. He was billed as the hero, I was the apprentice in waiting. My 12 goals to date seemed irrelevant, but that's football; it was something I would have to get used to, and quick.

Throughout the season I would keep a close eye on my England rivals, hoping they would continually have quiet games, but that is only natural. As soon as I'd walked off the pitch on a Saturday afternoon I wanted to know who had scored. I wanted that Euro 2000 spot, I wanted the Golden Boot. But I was pleased to see Michael back in action after the injury problems he'd had. I could empathize with him on that score.

Shearer and Cole would emerge as my main rivals for the top goalscorer's prize in 1999/2000, although I was shocked to see Chris Sutton having such a mediocre season. Having secured a dream move to Stamford Bridge, following an accomplished spell at Blackburn, I expected him to be challenging for the Golden Boot and an England spot. To score only one league all season was a sad indictment on a fine player, but it proved to be one of those seasons for him. You could sense in the opening game against us that it might not be his year as he missed three one-on-ones with Thomas Sorensen, treading on the ball twice and slipping over, too. If he'd scored one or two of those goals, it could have been a completely different outcome for him, although I'm sure he'll bounce back for Celtic in 2000/01.

Thankfully, I was not suffering a similar fate, although I did need the help of the Premier League panel following our game at Watford. There was no problem with my headed goal, but the other strike came via a wicked deflection off Mark Williams, which completely wrong-footed Alec Chamberlain. The shot was weak and in normal circumstances Alec would have put his cap on the ball, but I was claiming the goal all the same. Thankfully, Andy Gray is on the panel and as a fellow striker and close friend of Peter Reid's, I knew there would be only one outcome. The goal ultimately proved vital because without it, I would have ended the season on 29 goals and outside the exclusive 30 club, alongside Shearer and Cole.

I seemed to have a habit of scoring against Watford but I felt a great deal of sadness as they capitulated at the highest level. The step-up obviously came too quickly, so hopefully they can now re-assess the situation in Division One and renew their challenge again in the seasons to come.

We had a better grasp of Premier League life and still remained in the top five. The pinnacle of this rosy period in the season occurred against Chelsea at the Stadium of Light on 4 December. It was payback time for us following the resounding defeat at Stamford Bridge and we played as if we had so much to prove.

We were 4–0 up by half-time and I doubt whether this team will ever play so well again. Even Manchester United would have struggled to contain us, such was the magnitude of our performance. Quinny's opening goal in the first minute set the trend for the afternoon and it also provided the platform for my crowning moment of the season, a 25-yard strike which rates as my favourite goal of the season.

When I connected, I thought it was sailing way over the bar. But having hit the ball with the outside of my right foot, the flight was not true, and I could sense the ball dipping. Ed de Goey was also struggling to get near it and when the ball hit the back of the net, an incredible rush of emotion engulfed my body. I sprinted towards the dug out and slid on my knees along the turf, arms held aloft in celebration. I knew it would be our day. I also knew it was a goal which would elevate me to another level. It was against Chelsea, it was on *Match of the Day* and it would turn me into a national figure. I had scored goals all season, but I still felt I needed to score against a side of Chelsea's calibre to end all the doubts. I never did make a reference to Rodney Marsh and his comments on television when he said that I would struggle to score goals in the Premiership. I didn't need to. But it is a nice feeling to make people eat their own words.

But as we all know, football is full of peaks and troughs and having overcome Portsmouth in the FA Cup and Southampton in the league, our season would then disintegrate at an alarming pace.

CHAPTER ELEVEN

'If You Can't Keep
the Ball...'

Having suffered a slight hamstring strain in the build up to our Boxing Day trip to Everton, I was taken out of the firing line and can remember listening to the local radio at home as we fell 3–0 behind at half-time, before conceding another two in the second half. It was enough to make me choke on my Christmas dinner and it was heartbreaking to know that the lads were suffering.

In the post-match phone-in, many fans were saying the scoreline would have been different if I had played, but on speaking to the lads afterwards it was clear that every player had a below-par game and I doubt whether I would have made any difference. Kevin Kilbane, our new signing from West Brom, was asked to fill my boots but as a left winger, he was out of position and, unjustly, made a scapegoat. It would take him some time to win our fans over.

I was also absent for the big Sky game against Manchester United, a match I had been looking forward to all season. Although we went 2–0 up, you could sense United would come back into the game and it was no surprise when Nicky Butt equalised (even if it looked from my position that Ole Gunner Solskjaer earned the free-kick having been tackled by one of the hose outlets on the pitch!)

United had that never-say-die attitude which has become a trait of their success. Arsenal, Chelsea, Liverpool and Leeds may have been equally gifted in terms of personnel but none of them could match the consistency of United and they deserved their championship success. I do, however, believe it will be a much tighter race in 2000/01 and the aforementioned teams should all be pushing them much closer.

Wimbledon were proving to be our nemesis with another defeat as we moved into the new millennium, before we found ourselves embroiled in a controversy which would rage for days afterwards.

Tranmere were heading towards a 1–0 victory in our FA Cup fourth round clash at Prenton Park in January, but having seen Clint Hill receive his marching orders, we were given added impetus to make a final push for an equalizer. To take the sting out of the situation, Rovers sent on Stephen Frail for Andy Parkinson but, amazingly, the player did not leave the field as we prepared to take a free-kick. Rovers had eleven players on the pitch and it wasn't until the ball was cleared – from Parkinson, of all people – that referee Rob Harris realized the mistake he had made. It resulted in incredible scenes of confusion among the officials, uproar from our bench and pleas of innocence from the Tranmere staff.

Parkinson was eventually brought off but the arguments continued up the tunnel and in the referee's room after the game. Some might feel our protests were petty and unsporting, but rules are rules and they had clearly been breached. Tranmere found themselves at an unfair advantage at a critical moment in the game, with a place in the fifth round of the FA Cup at stake.

Despite an appeal to the FA, I knew the result would not be overturned. A replay would be seen as further condemnation of Harris, and he had probably suffered enough. It left us bowing out again at the hands of Rovers and I was left to rue a header which should have found the back of the net.

Winning becomes a habit, likewise losing, although breaking a sequence of defeats is far harder to achieve. Your confidence suffers, you become tentative when in possession of the ball and the crowd become tetchy. We had found ourselves in the middle of a terrible run of results and although I managed to keep my goalscoring run going, the team was struggling. Defeats would follow against championship-chasing Leeds and Arsenal, and certain sections of the crowd were calling for Peter Reid's head.

The game I had been looking forward to all season, a trip to my beloved Highbury, quickly turned into a nightmare as we were trounced 4–1. Outclassed and outplayed in every position, we caught The Gunners just as they were putting their end-of-season run together and I don't think a steam train could have stopped them that day. At least I had sampled the Marble Halls, and played on the Highbury turf – scant consolation indeed.

Although the calls from the terraces were not as savage as those experienced in my early days at the club, they were pretty vociferous, which did irritate me. As I've said many times, our fans are the best in the world but when the going gets tough, sometimes they don't help the situation. That's the only criticism I have of them but such are the expectation levels at the club, it's almost inevitable that they will voice their dissatisfaction.

The anger was not reserved for our own players. The return of Michael Bridges in a Leeds shirt was met with far greater contempt. A surprise to some, but he did himself no favours in the game at Elland Road by aiming gestures at our fans which certainly wasn't warranted.

It was fated that he would score but with a property in the area at the time, his celebration was certainly muted. His goal was just one of many he scored in the Premiership in 1999/2000 and his decision to leave was certainly justified.

Michael has proved his class at this level and I expect him to go from strength to strength. We had a little chat after the game and it was clear that he was relishing regular first team football. He had rediscovered his confidence and I was pleased for him.

He ended the season with 21 goals, and it was a great feat to break that 20-goal barrier. That was a landmark I was delighted to reach that same game, robbing Jonathan Woodgate of the ball before crashing a shot in off Nigel Martyn's right post. I had reached my target for the season and, incredibly, we were still in January.

If there was ever a game to help us break out of our rut, it was the return of Newcastle United. Much had happened on Tyneside since our last encounter: Gullit had departed, Bobby Robson had arrived and the side were playing with renewed vigour and were winning games.

From the opening encounters, you could see the Sunderland players were far more confident, the work rate higher and they were playing for a manager they respected. We did, in fact, start very poorly and deserved to go 2–0 down but it was imperative that we tried to claw ourselves back before half-time. I managed to score after 23 minutes and we went in at half-time 2–1 down, but we knew the scales were tipping in our balance.

The second half was one-way traffic as we launched an onslaught in front of our own fans. We had so many opportunities but the Toon goal seemed to lead a charmed life as chance after chance went begging. We felt it might not be our day when the prolific Chris Makin went close with two efforts, one of which shaved the bar.

But with the Sunderland masses urging us on in the electric atmosphere, we would not give up and we received our just desserts with just eight minutes left as I somehow bundled the ball home. The Newcastle players were appealing for offside but Dabizas was clearly playing me on and I just ran towards our fans in the far corner of the stadium. The feeling was even better than the goal I scored at St James', simply because I had scored at home. I remember a few fans came running towards me and I was greeted by the smell of stale beer and sweaty shirts. The elation on their faces will live with me forever.

But if that was the shot in the arm we needed to kick-start our season, we were very much mistaken. We would lose 3–2 at Coventry the following week, having gone 3–0 down at half-time, although we were unlucky not to come away with a point, having hit the post late on.

England's friendly with Argentina was a welcome relief from the traumas of club football and having scored 22 goals, I was confident Kevin Keegan would continue his experimentation in the build up to Euro 2000. It was patently clear that Shearer and Owen would, if fit, lead the country into the tournament, so I thought I might get my chance here in this friendly. Instead, Emile Heskey was thrust into the spotlight, putting in a sterling performance in the process. With his strength and power, Emile gives the manager another option and he won his place in the squad that night.

I did manage to get a run-out, for the final 13 minutes as a replacement for Shearer, making my Wembley bow. It's impossible to show what you can do in such a short space of time against such quality opposition, but I was just delighted to win another cap. Who knows, if we didn't having a major tournament fast approaching on the horizon, I might have had longer or even started the game.

My international despondency was not affecting my league form, though, as I scored in consecutive games against Leicester and Liverpool. It was now 25 goals for the season and I had put myself on a pedestal as the club's most prolific goalscorer of modern times. To celebrate the achievement, I was presented with a shirt by

Sunderland legend Brian Clough, whose goalscoring feats and records I am honoured to have matched.

The timing was certainly strange. Having come in against Middlesbrough at half-time, Peter told me to go back on to the pitch for the presentation. No disrespect, but at that moment in time, I just wanted to concentrate on the game. However, it was an absolute honour to meet Cloughie, although my residing memory is of a frail, poorly man who now looks a shadow of his former radiant self. He was gaunt, shaking and it was heartbreaking to see. He didn't say much, just a 'well done, son' but as we were posing for pictures, I remember him kicking the back of my leg. I wondered what he was doing at first, but it was his way of cracking a joke. It was a great moment in the season for me, and hopefully I'll be invited back in 20 or 30 years to greet the next Sunderland goalscoring hero.

Our sorry run of 12 games without a win was finally halted against the team who started the collapse, Everton. Another goal put me in a confident frame of mind going into the Southampton game – my first trip back to The Dell since I was sent packing all those years ago.

The overall appearance of the stadium had changed, with both ends now covered, but it remained as I remembered it – a tight, compact ground with an excellent playing surface. It was an emotional moment when I walked past the manager's room where I was given the fateful news all those years ago. It was then into the dressing room I used to clean and coming face to face with the astroturf floor that proved so difficult to clean.

I also saw one of my old coaches Dennis Rofe, as well as Jason Dodd, who had become the club's first-choice right-back, but not a lot was said. They all knew they'd made a mistake. But I could reminisce no more. I had a professional job to do and I so desperately wanted to add to my season's goal tally.

I had to wait 86 minutes, converting a penalty following a rash challenge on Kevin Kilbane, and having won 2–1 in consecutive games, the talk was again of Europe in training that week. We knew we would have to win our remaining home games to stand a chance, with tough away games at Manchester United, Sheffield Wednesday and Aston Villa to follow.

I couldn't wait to play at Old Trafford, having heard so much about the stadium. True, the arena is impressive but I was extremely disappointed with the atmosphere. There is no comparison with the noise our fans make, but maybe that's because the United fans have now become so used to winning games. Their passion might not be as strong – but I suppose when you're cruising to a 4–0 victory, maybe there is no need to get hyped up.

We were completely outplayed, a carbon-copy of the performance at Highbury, and both games showed the gulf between ourselves and the top two teams. It proved to be my toughest afternoon of the season, as I was shadowed by Jaap Stam for the full 90 minutes. He stood out as my most difficult opponent of the season, an immense figure. I broke free from his reins on just the one occasion, only for the Dutchman to haul me down. He was lucky to stay on the pitch and it could have been a different story if United had been reduced to ten men. Then again…

Victory at Hillsborough put us back on the UEFA trail, and my curled effort from the edge of the box rates among one of my favourite goals of the season. I scored two goals that afternoon to take me to 29 in total but, in truth, the performance was scrappy.

Our European ambitions finally succumbed at the hands of Bradford. The game was billed as the match to mark my 30th goal of the season but in all honesty, neither myself nor the team got out of second gear and we proceeded to lose 1–0. The champagne had to be put on ice but, fittingly, I would reach the landmark figure against West Ham in our final home game of the season.

There was no denying I had emerged from the shadows, from Division One striker to household figure in the space of 12 months. It proved incomprehensible for me at times, certainly when I was invited down to the *A Question of Sport* studios with Niall Quinn. As a lad, I used to watch all the stars pit their wits against each other on the show and only the cream of the crop in their respective fields are invited. I was now to join the select band and I must admit to feeling extremely nervous when I sat at the table with Quinny and John Parrott. Scoring goals comes naturally to me, but when you know millions will be watching at home, the perspiration creeps up under the studio lights. The show took two hours to record and what the viewers at home don't realize is that you are allowed up to 20 minutes to answer a question – or ask for help among your team-mates. I've let out a trade secret now, but my pre-show nerves were soon at ease as I answered my questions correctly. Steve Redgrave and Matthew Pinsent were comfortably brushed aside as the thick footballers overcame their university-educated counterparts.

Our partnership continued on the pitch as Quinny took our joint goals' tally to 43 for the season in the 1–1 draw at Aston Villa but the personal anxiety had now reached fever pitch.

As a few of us travelled down that evening to the PFA Awards dinner at the Grosvenor Hotel, I must admit that my mind was elsewhere on the journey to London. My fretting was, however, soon put to one side as we took our table and looked forward to the evening's entertainment.

As the second half of the season began to draw to a close, it became apparent that I would be in the running for the PFA Player of the Year Award and the Football Writers' equivalent. Although it was an honour to be nominated for both, the PFA award is the one I hold in the highest esteem as it's recognition from the people who matter – the players. I voted for Roy Keane, likewise most of the Sunderland players (you can't nominate club mates), so I knew I would probably have to vie for the runners-up spot with Harry Kewell and Sami Hyppia.

As the evening got underway at the Grosvenor, each player in the running was profiled on a giant video screen. My clip brought cheers from our table: Paul Butler, Andy Marriott, Quinny and Alex Rae. It brought a lump to my throat as the goal against Chelsea was replayed and for a few minutes, it really did feel as if I would take the top accolade.

That, of course, went to Keane but it was heartening to hear the Irishman say that I should have carried away the silverware instead of finishing second.

The after-show party – yes, Deech was the DJ – was held in the West End and I spent much of the evening catching up with my old mate Pagey, while discovering how Andy Melville and Kevin Ball were dealing with the bright lights of the city.

Sol Campbell also introduced me to my hero Ian Wright that night and having been so complimentary towards me in his *Sun* columns all season, I felt obliged to have a chat. We had followed similar paths to the top and it was great to meet the guy in the flesh and just talk football with him for a few minutes. He promised me I would break 30 goals and who was I to argue?

True to his word, I had to wait just one more week until my date with destiny. The game against West Ham was just 14 minutes old when Nick Summerbee propelled forward a typically accurate cross and as soon as the ball had left his foot, I knew I would connect with a header and the ball would nestle in the net. My instincts proved correct and the lid almost came off the stadium when the ball crossed the line. Thirty goals is an incredible achievement by anyone's standards, but to achieve such a feat in my first season of Premiership football is one I'm particularly proud of.

Alan Shearer stated that no player would again score 30 Premiership goals in a season, but I've proved the exception to the rule. I've also reached my tally at a time when the Premiership is stronger than ever. I'm not belittling Alan or Andy Cole's achievements, but the league certainly did not boast the high calibre of international defenders we now have in the game, back when they hit the magical figures.

Another Golden Boot, another successful season, another obstacle comfortably overcome.

Much was made of the BMW I had been promised by our chief executive John Fickling if I reached 30 goals. Having bumped into him in a BMW showroom early in the season, he promised he'd buy me one if I reached 35 goals but after some gentle persuasion by Julie, he settled on 30 goals. Never in my wildest dreams did I think I'd reach such a target but, true to his word, John has offered to buy me the car. But now I've signed a new contract, I have decided to give the equivalent money to the Sunderland Children's Hospice and the Sunderland Heart Foundation. It's my way of giving something back to a community who have supported me so vociferously these past three seasons.

The tremendous backing I've received was a major factor in my decision to sign a new five-year contract at the beginning of 2000. Having started the season so well and with interest from other clubs now more prominent, the club honoured a promise to improve my contract.

But I didn't create a commotion or place unfeasible demands on the board. I waited until Christmas, having scored 19 goals, before putting my case forward. The talks were very amicable between myself and the club but when your future is at stake, you can't rush into a decision. I have to admit there was a stage during the talks when I thought the situation could break down and the possibility of moving on seemed real, but when I took stock of the situation, I realized I'd be a fool to leave such a great club and a wonderful set of supporters.

This club is building for the future and I want to be a part of that. I am confident silverware will arrive at the Stadium of Light in the next two or three years and having worked so hard to get us into such a lofty position, I want to reap the benefits.

I finally put pen to paper in February and the contract I signed would probably not have been bettered had I moved on. The news was greeted with great relief from the fans, whose concerns were growing, and it alleviated a stressful period for me. I could now relax, concentrate on scoring goals for Sunderland and eventually cement my main aim for the season – a Euro 2000 squad place.

A critical point in the international calendar came with a showpiece game against Brazil at Wembley in May. With the domestic season now at its conclusion, I was hoping to channel all my energies into making the final squad. With Heskey having all but confirmed his place alongside Shearer and Owen and with Robbie Fowler a firm favourite of Keegan, it would be a straight fight between myself and Andy Cole to make the plane to Holland and Belgium.

I was the man in form and the man on the minds of the public, having ended the season with my selective pots of silverware. It was encouraging to hear so many fans across the country declaring their support for me, but there was only one man whose opinion counted and, it appeared, he thought otherwise.

I would feature for just six minutes of the Brazil game, replacing goalscorer Owen, and with the squad set to be announced four days later prior to the Ukraine fixture, I felt I'd missed the boat. I thought my dream was coming to an end, and I just wanted to get onto the pitch, do my best and earn another cap. Despite my disillusionment, it was an education to see the Brazilians at such close quarters. Technically they were superb and from the centre-halves to the strikers, they were all competent on the ball. You couldn't fault our work rate and commitment as we came away with a 1–1 draw, but as would be proved, you need much more if you want to excel at the highest level.

Frustration had engulfed me and I let my emotions get the better of me after the match by outpouring my anxieties to the press. Andy Cole had been declared fit following his ongoing toe problem, and I honestly thought the end was nigh. Some of the headlines were blown out of all proportion but I really was feeling low. In hindsight, it was unprofessional of me to vent my frustrations via the media, but I'll learn from such mistakes in the future.

Although the squad was announced after the Ukraine game, the players were to be informed on the afternoon of the match. Of course I was expecting the worst but as the match got ever nearer, I had heard nothing. My selection was confirmed via a process of elimination. The only players the boss would speak to were those left behind. News eventually filtered through that Andy Cole had already left for Manchester and it was at that moment that I knew I had made it.

A massive weight had been lifted from my shoulders in an instant, although I must admit it was a real surprise to see Andy pull out with an injury. He appeared to be running freely in training and had declared himself fit, but following a chat with Kevin he must have felt the injury wasn't worth risking in such an important tournament and that he wouldn't do himself justice. I did not feature in the game that night, but at least I could relax a little. Both my goals for the season had been attained: 20 goals for Sunderland and a place in the Euro 2000 squad. A smile had, at last, returned to my face.

Malta was the venue for our final warm-up game and I assumed the match would be a dress rehearsal for our opening group game with Portugal nine days later. But this game never ceases to surprise me, and I was honoured to finally make the side. I also saw it as an encounter in the last chance saloon. No matter how much hard work and endeavour you put in during a game, a striker is judged on his goals and with semi-professional opposition, I knew I had to break my duck if I was to prove worthy of at least a run-out during the tournament itself.

I had one great chance when I rounded the keeper, only to find the side-netting. I also had a goal disallowed for offside. If either of them had gone in, I could have scored two or three, but it again showed the thin line between success and failure at this level.

I was substituted after an hour and replaced by Robbie Fowler but few players could come out with a clear conscience in a very lacklustre performance. Heskey and Martin Keown saved our blushes in a 2–1 win, not the best of preparation for such a big tournament.

Another chance had slipped through my fingers but,

again, I found myself replaced as I was starting to get to grips with the pace of the game and the intense Valetta heat. Unlike many of the players, I had not played a full 90 minutes for three weeks and it was taking time to rediscover my sharpness. I was just pleased to return to the confines of the north east for a couple of days, as we'd been away as a team for two weeks now.

Euro 2000, itself, went very quickly and our base, the Balmoral Golf and Country Club, had the facilities to occupy our minds when the football had stopped. From a cinema club to pinball, pool, tennis, golf and a specialized assembled arcade area, there was little chance for boredom. The invention of DVD has also been a godsend, as the players swapped films throughout the tournament.

Of course you had cliques among the squad, that's only natural in such a big group, but I can honestly say it was a happy camp and everyone appeared to enjoy each other's company. I developed a close affinity with Ipswich keeper Richard Wright, possibly due to our Division One backgrounds, and if you could win tournaments for togetherness and camaraderie, we would have won hands down. The reality, however, was much different.

Kevin Keegan had stated to the media that we could win the tournament, having endured such a difficult path to the finals. The players felt exactly the same, otherwise there would have been no point in turning up, and after 20 minutes of our opening game against Portugal in Eindhoven, there was a certain justification in his words.

But although I did not feel Portugal would win, I could

sense they might at least get a draw from the game as we sat back and they stepped up two gears. Luis Figo's deflected goal could have gone anywhere, but it nestled into the back of David Seaman's net and from that moment on, they were in the ascendancy.

Nuno Gomes' winning goal came as a result of further poor defending of the ball and from 2–0 up we were facing defeat firmly in the face. The final whistle was greeted with much derision from the England supporters and although I could understand their frustration, the abuse handed out to David Beckham and a couple of other players, as we headed back down the tunnel, was a disgrace. We have all received insults as professional players but when it is aimed at your family, we are entering new territory. The vitriol aimed at David was particularly disgraceful and I just hope that those responsible have been dealt with severely and will never have the chance to watch another England game.

The backlash in the press was inevitable but I doubt whether Portugal will ever play that way again. However, they certainly taught us a lesson in tactics and technical composure and we would be foolish not to learn from the situation.

The Germany game was a one-off, a Premiership game if you will. Full of blood, thunder and endeavour, it wasn't pleasing to the eye, or to us watching from the bench, but three points lifted so many years of hurt and, more importantly, the 1–0 win set us up nicely for the final group game against Romania.

We all know the circumstances surrounding that particular defeat. In fact, it was a carbon-copy of the

Portugal game. We took our chances but we were technically inferior and stuck in our rigid 4-4-2 ways. Phil Neville took the brunt of abuse for his last-minute mistimed tackle, but we lost the match as a team over 90 minutes.

Back in the changing room, Kevin's dressing down was short and to the point. 'If you can't keep the ball or pass the ball, you don't deserve to go through' he said. Simple enough, but so true.

We left the tournament knowing our passing and technique needed drastic improvement, from junior football upwards. Some people have questioned Kevin Keegan's position as head coach but I don't think there's a better man for the job. He gets the best out of his players, has great motivational skills and he admits he's still learning. That's amazing to think, considering everything he achieved as a player and as Newcastle's manager, but I'm certain he will get it right in the end.

Naturally it was very disappointing not to at least appear from the subs' bench. In any other team in the world, if a player had scored 30 goals in their domestic season, they would be a certainty for their national side. Unfortunately, we have so many quality centre-forwards to chose from at the moment, Kevin opted for experience rather than form.

In fact, there was no moment throughout the duration of the tournament that I felt I would play. Heskey was Kevin's preferred third option and then I felt as if Robbie Fowler would be chosen ahead of me. Kevin could sense my disappointment in training, he's not stupid, and he kept telling me to 'keep training hard, keep mentally focused' although at times, that seemed very difficult to comprehend. I just felt unwanted, as if I was there solely for the ride.

That was Kevin's prerogative to keep me on the sidelines, but in hindsight, maybe it was the best thing that could have happened to me. I was excused by the media from our poor performances in Euro 2000 and the calls for my inclusion have heightened ever since. I know I am good enough to play at this level and I am determined to show Kevin in the coming months that I am worthy of a starting place in his team.

The retirement of Alan Shearer has certainly helped my cause although many people feel Heskey is his natural successor. When you put Emile's attributes alongside that of a prolific goalscorer, you have a great partnership and I would certainly relish playing alongside him.

But Kevin also has the option of a smaller partnership, with myself, Michael, Robbie and Andy falling into that category. This would also encourage balls played into feet and provide the catalyst to a more 'continental' style of football that we so yearn for in this country.

Whatever happens, there is certainly much for me to play for at international level but I know, like my striking counterparts, that I will not get anywhere unless I perform for my club.

That's the aim again this season, to continue scoring goals for Sunderland and once again break my target of 20 goals for the season.

I'm under no illusion that it will be much harder for me this time round, as I will be a marked man. But I've been working extra hard in training on my speed of thought, my positioning and my shooting. I'm continually striving to be the best and I know that if the chances are being created for me, I'll continue to score goals.

I've yet to experience a barren spell as a Sunderland player but when the inevitable happens, I'll just keep reiterating the point that I have proved myself as a prolific Premiership striker. I can score goals at this level and I will score goals for England.

The personal accolades are on my mantelpiece at home – the latest being the European Golden Boot, which I won ahead of Jardel and Van Nistelrooy. It's such a prestigious honour to have won the award, following in the footsteps of great footballing names such as Eusebio and Karl-Heinz Rumminegge. Now it's time for Sunderland to start making inroads, too. Naturally, our aim this season is to cement our Premiership place and to sustain a run in one of the cups. To appear in an FA Cup or League Cup final would be fantastic and would open up a place in Europe for us. In all honesty, I still think Europe is a bit premature but then again, who knows what set-up we might have at the club a few months down the line? A year ago, who would have thought we would have had such a tremendous season in the Premiership? Who would have thought I would score 30 goals? It's been an achievement attained by skill, determination and a desire to prove the doubters wrong.

Those three attributes have served me so well so far and, I am confident, will take me to even greater levels in the forthcoming seasons.

Career Highlights

Kevin Phillips

Born: Hitchin, 25 July 1973
Family: Dad Ray, Mum Sue,
Sisters Debbie, Tina,
Tricia, Karen
Height: 5ft 7in
Weight: 11st 2lb

Schools:
Trotts Hill Junior School
(Stevenage),
Collenswood Secondary School
(Stevenage)

Junior Football Clubs:
Derby Way Wanderers
(Stevenage),
Fairlands (Stevenage),
St Joseph's (Luton)

Professional Football Clubs:
Southampton, Watford,
Sunderland.
Turned YTS at Southampton 1
July 1988.
Turned Pro at Watford 12
December 1994.

Club Record
1994-95   Watford
Appearances(and goals)
League: 16(9)
FA Cup: 0
Coca-Cola Cup: 0

1995-96   Watford
League: 27(11)
FA Cup: 2(0)
Coca-Cola Cup: 2(1)

1996-97 Watford
League: 15(4)
FA Cup: 0
Coca-Cola Cup: 0

1997-98 Sunderland
League: 43(29)
FA Cup: 2(4)
Coca-Cola Cup: 0

Honours
Nationwide Player of the Year
SHOOT/Adidas Golden Boot
    winner
Sunderland Supporters Player of
    the Year
Sunderland Echo Player of the
    Year
North East Football Writers
    Player of the Year runner-up
Sunderland Internet Site Player
    of the year
Nationwide Player of the
    Month (Jan)
Sunderland Echo Player of the
    Month (Nov, Dec, Jan, April)

1998-99 Sunderland
League: 26(23)
FA Cup: 1(0)
Worthington Cup: 5(2)

Honours
Nationwide Player of the
Month (March)
Sunderland Echo Player of the
Month (Jan)

1999-2000 Sunderland
League: 36(30)
FA Cup: 2(0)
Worthington Cup: 0(0)

Honours
Premier League Golden Boot
Carling Player of the Year
European Golden Boot Winner
PFA Player of the Year –
    Runner-up
Football Writers' Player of the
    Year – Runner-up
Sunderland Player of the Year
Sunderland Supporters' Player
    of the Year

International Record
1997-98   England B: 1(0)
1998-99   England Full: 1(0)
1999-2000 England Full: 4(0)

Index